UNAUTHORIZED

D0493827

UNAUTHORIZED

SUE CRAWFORD

MICHAEL O'MARA BOOKS LIMITED

First published in Great Britain in 2002 by
Michael O'Mara Books Limited
9 Lion Yard, Tremadoc Road
London SW4 7NQ

This edition first published in 2003

Copyright © 2002, 2003 Michael O'Mara Books Limited

All rights reserved. No part of this publication may be
reproduced, stored in a retrieval system, or transmitted
by any means, without the prior permission in writing of
the publisher, nor be otherwise circulated in any form of
binding or cover other than that in which it is published
and without a similar condition including this condition
being imposed on the subsequent purchaser.

The right of Sue Crawford to be identified as the author
of this work has been asserted by her in accordance with
the Copyright, Designs and Patents Act 1988.

A CIP catalogue record for this book is available
from the British Library

ISBN 1-84317-016-7

1 3 5 7 9 10 8 6 4 2

Designed and typeset by Martin Bristow

Colour plates sections designed by www.glensaville.com

Printed and bound in Great Britain by Cox & Wyman, Reading, Berks

Contents

Author's Acknowledgments

THANKS TO EVERYONE who assisted with the compilation of this biography, in particular author Andrew Morton and photographer Ken Lennox for their help and guidance, and Rick Sky for his memories and insight into life on the road with Ozzy. Others generously gave their time but would prefer to remain anonymous; their help was also appreciated.

At Michael O'Mara Books I would like to thank Michael O'Mara for commissioning the book, my editor Karen Dolan, Editorial Director Gabrielle Mander and Managing Editor Toby Buchan for their enthusiasm and support, Judith Palmer for her tireless picture research, and Rhian McKay for her patient and thorough research. I am grateful too to Diana Briscoe for compiling the discography and chronology, to Dominique Enright for the Index and to Adrian Morris for preparing Ozzy's birthchart. Thanks are also due to Martin Bristow for the book's excellent design, and to Glen Saville for the stunning picture section.

Finally, thanks to Ozzy Osbourne for living such a 'fucking' incredible life, for giving his time so generously to so many journalists for interviews over the years and giving pleasure to millions, including me.

Also a heartfelt thank you to Sharon Osbourne for keeping Ozzy alive for the last eight chapters; without her this would have been a very slim volume.

SUE CRAWFORD
February 2003

RECOMMENDED READING/LISTENING

Diary of a Madman by Mick Wall, published by Zomba Books
Black Sabbath by Steven Rosen, published by Sanctuary
    Publishing
Paranoid by Mick Wall, published by Mainstream Publishing
Black Sabbath: The Ozzy Osbourne Years by Robert V Conte with
    C J Henderson, published by Studio Chikara
The Rockview Interviews: Ozzy Osbourne, CD, published by
    Rockview Records
Maximum Ozzy – The Unauthorised Biography of Ozzy Osbourne,
    CD, published by Chrome Dreams

foreword

John Michael Osbourne

❝ *Whatever else I do, my epitaph will be*
OZZY OSBOURNE
BORN DECEMBER 3, 1948.
DIED, WHENEVER.
AND HE BIT THE HEAD
OFF A BAT. ❞

IT MAY BE what he will always be best remembered for, but John 'Ozzy' Osbourne has come a long way since that infamous night back in 1982 when he bit the head off a live bat on stage in Des Moines, Iowa. Today, twenty years later, he is experiencing the highest profile ever in his remarkable thirty-three-year career. Playing before the Queen at Buckingham Palace, invited by President Bush to the White House, a chat-show favorite and natural raconteur and the star of his own docu-soap *The Osbournes*, he is one of the few people from heavy rock to have successfully crossed over into the mainstream.

Yet somehow, despite it all, he has still not become respectable. He may now be worth $85.5 million (£57 million) and live in a huge house in Beverly Hills, but he is not and never will be one of rock's establishment; a man who can safely be wheeled out at smart events to meet dignitaries and say the right thing. Ozzy will never be that. At Ozzfest every year he still plays to the same audience of rebellious teenagers as he started out life entertaining when he lived in the back streets of Birmingham. They love him precisely because he can't be trusted. Precisely because he still is so unpredictable. Yet it is those contrasts – the fact that he can appeal to two such diverse groups – that is the key to his incredible success. That he can at the same time play both the clown Prince and the Prince of Darkness and still remarkably be himself.

At times, over the years, Ozzy has been capable of the most appalling acts – biting the head off bats and doves,

11

urinating on the Alamo, snorting ants, cheating on his wives and imbibing every drug known to man. He is a man who once set fire to his house for fun, who emptied a shotgun into his car, who crashed another by driving it into a hedge and who risked his life driving at 100mph, without a license, after several bottles of brandy. His legendary career has provided vicarious thrills for generations of fans, as faced with opportunities for excess, Ozzy did what any true rocker would and embraced them all.

As Ozzy himself once explained: 'I'm a guy that can't take a fucking pill, I've got to take fifteen. I can't have a drink, I've got to get bombed. I've got to take everything to the end.' Even today, with the drugs long gone and the drink more or less under control, he still has the air of a rebel. He is rarely seen in public without his trademark round tinted sunglasses, and several large crosses and an eyeball hang on chains around his neck. His wardrobe typically consists of black t-shirts and jackets and even at home there is little change; to relax he simply slips into one of his forty pairs of black drawstring sweat pants.

But through all the wildness there is another, softer side to him. He is a devoted family man and his children mean the world to him. His first phone call after leaving the Betty Ford Clinic at Rancho Mirage in California in 1984 was to Jessica, his eleven-year-old daughter from his marriage to first wife Thelma. 'I'm straight now babe,' he told her. 'I'm sober and I'm never going to drink again.' It is a source of great sorrow to him that Jessica, now a thirty-one-year-old surveyor, will no longer speak to him, and his latest album contains a song about the pain he still feels over their estrangement. He is immensely proud of his son Louis, twenty-eight, also from his first marriage, who quit his job as a chef to become a successful club DJ. He still lives in England, but to Ozzy's delight is a regular visitor to his LA home. After years of having contact with only one of his sisters, all three – Jean, Iris and Gillian – were with Ozzy when he was awarded his star on the Hollywood Walk of Fame.

He is a remarkably generous man, once impulsively splashing out more than $14,500 (£10,000) at Tiffany in New York on diamond, ruby and emerald studded earrings for his entire road crew. He is also a genuine home bird, a man who relaxes by painting and watching television. A man truly appalled by the show business lifestyle, who stays away from nightclubs and other celebrities because he genuinely believes he has nothing in common with them – a request to play with Michael Jackson last year met with risible derision. A man whose favorite album is Paul McCartney's *Band on the Run*, a man whose favorite song is John Lennon's 'Imagine' – he and Sharon fell in love to it – a man whose record collection contains middle-of-the-road music such as Phil Collins, UB40 and Boy George.

The list could go on. Because the wild bat-eating Ozzy is actually only a tiny facet of his extraordinary personality. As Ozzy himself says: 'People think that I live in a dungeon with fucking vampires and bats, which is not the case, I'm just a normal person, it's just a role that I play.' How much of his life has been role-playing and how much has been real is not clear. Somewhere along the road the boundaries became blurred, to the public certainly, but perhaps also to Ozzy himself. Maybe, as he insists, it is just a role, but if it is, it has always been a role based on his personality. As pop commentator Rick Sky says: 'Ozzy is someone who is true to himself. You meet some artists who fake things and pretend that they're much wilder than they are. Ozzy is the genuine article and he wouldn't be like that if he didn't enjoy boozing and taking drugs, but at the same time you also get the feeling that he's caught in the myth. It's what fans want and he has to do that stuff. We like people that we can live vicariously through and Ozzy is willing to do all kinds of things. At school he would be the sort of guy that people would egg on to do things and he would do it and then get caught and punished.'

Certainly Ozzy has been punished over the years. Not just by the courts, but also by the toll his lifestyle has taken on his body. Yet his frailties and insecurities only serve to make him more human to us. And the fact that he never takes himself too seriously – his self-deprecating sense of humor is legendary – makes us love him all the more.

He is a bright man, more intelligent than he lets on, yet few would dispute that much of his present-day success is down to his wife Sharon. In 1979 she rescued him from the gutter and, at the same time, saved him from an early grave. She didn't try to change him; instead she has spent the past twenty-five years channeling his unique talents in yet more new directions. It was Sharon who took a man with a distinctive, yet no more than average voice and turned it into one of the most recognizable sounds in rock. It was Sharon who masterminded Ozzfest, Sharon who introduced Ozzy to a whole new generation of rock fans and Sharon who realized that his charisma and humor could make him a soap star who would appeal to every generation – mums, dads, fashionable thirty-somethings, teenagers and kids.

Yet all Sharon could do was mold what was already there. Nobody in their wildest dreams could have invented an Ozzy Osbourne. A man as mad as they come, yet still down to earth. A man who feels duty bound to play up and entertain, yet a man who is ironically enjoying a rebirth with *The Osbournes* for doing precisely the opposite – for simply being himself. A man who started out as nothing in a run-down house in the suburbs of Birmingham, England. A man who came into music straight from jail and without it would probably have gone straight back. Rags-to-riches do not begin to sum it up.

At fifty-four Ozzy remains a man of fascinating, immense contradictions. A middle-aged dad who is genuinely shocked by his teenage children's errant ways, yet a man who admits his favorite word is 'Fuck'. He might seem to have settled down, but as with a sleeping lion you wouldn't want to go too near and prod him with a stick. He endlessly enthralls us, because it is almost impossible to predict what he will do next. Quiet retirement? Or another thirty years of sex, drugs and rock 'n' roll? Whatever happens, nothing will surprise us. On a recent shopping trip to buy a cat-litter tray in LA, the assistant handed Ozzy his purchase with a cheery 'Enjoy!' Said the puzzled Prince of Darkness afterwards: 'What did she think I was going to do? Eat the cats?' Probably not, but with Ozzy you just never quite know . . .

chapter one

Backstreet Boy

❝ *You hear your mother crying because she has no dough to feed you. Or my father and her always fighting over something. And I used to sit on the front steps all the time and think, "One of these days I'm going to buy a Rolls-Royce and drive them out of this shithole". And I did it.* ❞

H IS WORKMATES SMILED sympathetically as the scrawny sixteen-year-old set about his gruesome task with gusto. Killing 250 cattle a day and cutting the guts out of sheep would be no ordinary teenager's idea of an ideal job, and the men could only assume that the enthusiasm of the latest recruit to the Digbeth abattoir stemmed from a desperate desire to escape the grinding poverty he had clearly grown up in.

They could have had no idea just how wrong their assumptions were. For the young man standing before them was no ordinary teenager. He had been no ordinary child, and he would go on to become one of the most extraordinary men of his generation. No ordinary teenager, after all, would have stabbed his aunt's cat at the age of just eleven. No ordinary teenager would have tried to hang himself with a clothesline at the age of fourteen, or tried to set his sister on fire by pouring petrol over her dress. And, certainly, no ordinary teenager would have enjoyed the bloody task of cutting open dead animals and sweeping up entrails for a living.

His abattoir experience might explain why, many years later, Ozzy Osbourne took such enormous delight in pelting his audiences with raw meat and the stomach-churning leftovers from butchers' shops, including innards and intestines. But back in the harsh post-war years in Midlands Britain, such fascinations were not a sign of showbiz excess, but of a troubled young man. A young man who had endured more in his first sixteen years than many people experience in a lifetime.

John Michael Osbourne came kicking and screaming in to the world weighing 10lbs 14oz on 3 December 1948. He was born not in hospital, but, as was the custom in the 1940s, was delivered by a midwife in one of the two small bedrooms of the place that was to be his home throughout his childhood – 14 Lodge Road in Aston, a gray suburb of Birmingham, England.

His father John, known to his family and friends as Jack, worked nights in the GEC steel plant as a toolmaker, while his mother Lillian worked days in the Lucas car plant assembling electrical circuits. Young Ozzy was the fourth of six children; he had three older sisters – Jean, Iris and Gillian – and two younger brothers – Paul and Tony. Aston in those days was a close-knit working-class area – neighbors left their doors open, there was trust and a helping hand and everyone knew each other. The people had pride, the front steps to their houses were scrubbed clean on a daily basis, but there was little money to go round. For the five years of World War Two, Birmingham had been a regular target for Hitler's German bombers, and when young Ozzy was born postwar food rations were still in force. Aston was a bleak industrial area, full of ball-bearing factories, foundries and beer companies and, while the local factories provided some work, the pay was poor and living conditions for many were atrocious. Travel was unheard of and it would be eleven years before Ozzy would even see the sea, and even then just once, on a visit to his Aunty Ada's in Sunderland. It would be an even longer time before the Osbourne clan was invited back. The day of the visit had been sunny, and Ozzy's mum took the opportunity for a spot of sunbathing in the backyard. Bored with watching his mother lying there motionless, Ozzy began to chase his aunt's cat around the yard, eventually stabbing it with a kitchen knife when he caught hold of it. His furious parents asked him what on earth had possessed him. Not for the first time Ozzy was unable to explain.

With such a large family, the Osbourne house was cramped and money was tight. The six children had no choice but to rub along – sharing the same bed. There were rarely clean sheets and the children would have to huddle up together, often putting overcoats over the bed to keep them warm in winter. There was no indoor plumbing, so during the night the children would pee in a bucket left at the end of the bed. The children never bothered, and their mum and dad were so busy that the bucket could often sit there un-emptied for weeks. With little money to go round, the children were dressed in hand-me-downs, but, as the first boy, Ozzy's clothes tended to be new. Not that it meant he ever had anything remotely like a full wardrobe – in an interview years later, he told how as a child he had only ever owned one pair of shoes, one pair of socks, one pair of pants, one shirt and a jacket. Like many poor children in those days, he would often go without underwear.

Struggling to hold down a job and bring up six children in grinding poverty meant his mother was permanently exhausted. His father sought refuge in drink and darts at the local pub, but when he did come back there would be frequent rows over the lack of money. 'There were a lot of arguments. Father worked in a factory and would come home hacking up his lungs, my mother worked in a factory. Money was short. We never had a lot. We had no expectations,' remembers Ozzy. In fits of rage his father would also beat his mother from time to time. As a man, Ozzy would copy what he had witnessed, using violence against both his wives, Thelma and Sharon. 'Until I woke up one day and thought, "this is so fucking wrong". But you are what your parents make you.' It was a harsh life and Ozzy used his imagination to escape. He loved television shows such as *I Love Lucy*, *Lassie* and *Roy Rogers*. But the darkness that was to plague him in later years was already present, and there were strange flights of fantasy, too, in which he would develop bizarre obsessions. He began to hear voices; on one occasion they told him to kill his mother and he also became convinced that his father would die in his sleep. His father worked nights so would sleep during the day, and young Ozzy would sit watching him for hours, convinced that he was actually dead.

At the age of seven, Ozzy went to the local primary school, Prince Albert Road Juniors. Soccer – a fascination for most young boys in England at that age – held no interest for him and schoolwork even less so, and Ozzy began to escape more and more into the depths of his increasingly eccentric imagination. In school breaks he would organize hanging squads, where he and his mates would find an old piece of rope, grab an unsuspecting victim and then 'hang' him from the roof of the toilets. His morbid fascination with death extended to his own family – he once tried to strangle one of his brothers, as well as attempting to set fire to one of his sisters. At the age of fourteen came the attempt to try to hang himself, using his mother's clothesline, in the back alley behind the family home. Ozzy made a noose, put the rope over the bar at the entrance to the back gate, climbed up on to a chair and jumped. He was saved only by his father wandering into the backyard and catching him in the act. A teenager today would be given sympathy and sent to a counselor to try to find out the cause of such misery. As Ozzy himself later confirmed, he was indeed an unhappy child: 'I was running on fear all the time'. But this was Birmingham in the early 1960s. And in a tough working-class city in those days, such desperate acts were not interpreted as cries for help, but as wilful naughtiness. Ozzy was soundly beaten – not for the first or last time.

On one occasion, bored with their usual games, Ozzy and his friends gave his brother a used condom and told him it was a balloon. His brother went into the house with the condom blown up and his father, horrified at the sight before him, washed the boy's mouth out with soap. When his father found out Ozzy was behind the prank, he was in trouble once more. Ozzy recalls: 'Basically I was a very private child. I'm a very private person now, but I was eccentric as a child in the respect that although I want to remain private, when I'm cornered, when I'm surrounded by a lot of other people, I feel I have to be an eccentric for them to like me.'

At the age of eleven, Ozzy moved to Birchfield Road Secondary Modern School in the nearby Birmingham suburb of Perry Barr. It was here that he picked up the nickname that was to stay with him for life – Ozzy, short for his surname Osbourne. For some children, school can be a blissful escape from the hardships and misery at home. For Ozzy, though, secondary school simply meant more misery. He played truant constantly, and on one of the rare occasions he did attend class, attacked a teacher with an iron bar. 'I hated school. It was so fucking frustrating, not being able to understand what they were trying to teach me. I had dyslexia and what they now call attention deficit disorder. My children have it too; we live in California so they can go to a special school. I would get by in class by clowning around.'

The only subject the young Ozzy was any good at was music, and he took part in a variety of school opera plays, including Gilbert and Sullivan's *HMS Pinafore*, *The Mikado* and the *Pirates of Penzance*. He had inherited his love of music from his mother, who sang in local talent competitions. 'My mother was an amateur singer, my father was an amateur drunk,' he later dryly recalled. One of his earliest memories was of family get-togethers at home, involving huge singsongs. And he has similar recollections of his father returning from the local pub after a few beers, giving his children raucous renditions of traditional British pub songs, such as

'Show Me The Way To Go Home' and 'My Old Man'. Many Sunday afternoons were spent with other young boys his age sitting outside the local pub, waiting for the dads to come home. He could hear the voices of the men singing, growing louder and louder with every beer they downed. And with each rendition, Ozzy grew more and more enthraled.

But music wasn't to be the only influence he received from those visits to the pub. By the time he was twelve, his dad would take him into the pub with him and buy him half a pint of beer mixed with lemonade. Ozzy hated the taste, but was fascinated by the effect the drink would have on his dad. 'He'd just had a big row with my mum at home, he's pissed off, but ten minutes later he's singing 'The Old Mill By The Stream'. I'd try and imagine what the booze must be like. I thought it must be like the best lemonade in the world,' Ozzy recalled later. When he himself began drinking a few years later, Ozzy hated the taste of beer initially, but enjoyed the sensation of intoxication that it gave. 'So I'd just tip it down until I got the feeling,' he recalled.

By now Ozzy was listening to his first rock and roll records. American stars, such as Chuck Berry, Elvis Presley and Gene Vincent, were being played on the radio in Britain and his older sisters were bringing home their records and playing them on his parents' rickety old record player. For youngsters brought up listening to the rather sedate sounds of their parents' wartime Big Band records, it was an exciting time. But Ozzy's love of music was to make him an instant target for the taunts of his classmates, including one particular boy who singled him out, Tony Iommi. Ironically, the two boys would later reunite to form Black Sabbath, but back then they were from different gangs and there was no love lost between them. Tony and his friends would make fun of Ozzy's high voice and the two would end up brawling on many occasions.

By the age of fourteen, the thrill of the formal operatic music of Gilbert and Sullivan had begun to pale and Ozzy formed his own group, The Black Panthers. He was already getting into trouble at school for ditching his uniform of black shoes and gray flannels for jeans and the footwear favored by British teenage 'bad' boys – 'winkle-pickers' (pointed-toed shoes). At night, to his mother's horror, he was slipping out to enjoy the bad boy lifestyle, spending hours in cafés and coffee bars, playing pool and sneaking behind the coal shed to enjoy an illicit packet of cigarettes with friends.

But the 'Teds', as the youths were known, were never really Ozzy's thing. Just like hanging out at the canal and hurling bricks into the water, or wandering through the nearby cornfields and setting fire to barns, becoming a Ted was a convenient way of whiling away the hours and keeping the boredom at bay, but the life didn't really move him or inspire him. It wasn't until Ozzy was fourteen and he heard the strains of The Beatles' first single 'Love Me Do' that he finally found what he had been looking for. He was blown away. While he had enjoyed the rock and roll music of the 50s, it had never captured his imagination quite like Paul, John, George and Ringo. He took on part-time jobs, a newspaper round, a grocery delivery round and another job humping sacks of coal – anything to get together the money to buy copies of The Beatles' follow-up singles, 'Please Please Me' and 'From Me To You', as soon as they hit the shops. If he didn't have the money, he would simply hide the record under his coat and run. The songs were like nothing anyone in Britain had ever heard before, but it wasn't just the music that inspired Ozzy. The rock and rollers of the 50s had mainly been Americans. But The Beatles were four ordinary working-class British youngsters from Liverpool. They had come from the backstreets and hit the big time, and their success made Ozzy realize his own dreams were possible too. 'I was never a big fan of anyone in particular,' he says. 'But when The Beatles came along it turned my head. My wall was full of Beatles pictures. I used to fantasize about a Beatle marrying one of my sisters.'

Ozzy's love of The Beatles, however, only made him the target of more abuse from Tony Iommi and his gang. One morning in school break, they caught fifteen-year-old Ozzy singing 'I Want To Hold Your Hand' to himself. While the gang circled the defenseless schoolboy, chanting, 'Oz-brain! Oz-brain!' Tony punched and kicked him. After the beating, Ozzy swore he would join the Royal Air Force so he would never have to encounter Tony again.

This turned out to be nothing more than an idle threat and, when he calmed down, Ozzy returned to his private fantasies of screaming fans and millions in the bank. But such ambitions were still a long way off. To all intents and purposes, his group The Black Panthers were an imaginary band. They never played live and it's doubtful they even owned any instruments, but Ozzy wasn't in the least put off. Far from it. In his mind at least he was as big as The Beatles and he proudly wandered around Aston, adding his band's name to the graffiti-strewn walls. Even today, Ozzy claims he can take you to a wall that carries the name Black Panthers, along with other bits of his graffiti, such as Ozzy – Iron Man and Iron Maiden. This was long before Black Sabbath got together, and over a decade before the formation of Iron Maiden, but Ozzy's imagination was way ahead of his time.

By now Ozzy was desperate to leave school, but, while his heart was full of dreams of musical success, his head was briefly to rule his heart. His parents' financial situation was still as fraught as ever and Ozzy wanted to help them out. For all his wayward behavior, he adored his mum and dad and knew they were giving him everything they possibly could. In his eyes, it was now his turn to pay them back and, when asked on a school survey what his ambition was, he wrote that he wanted to become a plumber. It was a simple ambition and a practical one; he knew it was achievable and he knew it would mean instant money. In 1963, at the age of fifteen, he quit school. He worked briefly in a series of jobs – in a factory and laboring on a building site, before he finally persuaded a local plumber to take him on as his assistant. But it was winter and most of the work was outside in the freezing cold. Ozzy was miserable and stuck it out for as long as he could, but quickly realized that it was not the job for him. He quit and became a toolmaker's apprentice, but only months later he was on the move again – this time the local slaughterhouse beckoned. He stayed there for two years and it was to be the longest he would ever hold down a regular job. 'I loved killing animals,' he later recalled. 'It was definitely my forte. I used to stick them, stab them, chop them, totally torture the fuckers to death. And if the pigs had worms I used to bite their heads off. Even back then the people I worked with thought I was mad, too outrageous.'

A psychiatrist could have a field day with Ozzy's obsession with blood and gore – the contrast between the quietly spoken music-loving young man he could be, and the wild monster that often escaped. It is a dichotomy that has haunted him throughout his life, but even Ozzy isn't sure where exactly his fascination with the dark side came from. Certainly he endured a difficult childhood, but Ozzy has always been at pains to make it clear that his dark and wild side was never the fault of his mum and dad – far from it. 'My parents gave me all they could, but it was never enough for me,' he once explained. 'I wanted everything I could lay my hands on. I wanted to be Superman; I wanted to be the devil. And I always had a big thing about the darker side of life, the morbid gray side of things.'

Not all things dark amused Ozzy back then, though. In particular, rats horrified him; the slaughterhouse was full of them and, to this day, Ozzy still has a phobia about them. Then there were the pranks his workmates would play on the new employee. One day they filled his pockets with offal and Ozzy, unaware of the joke, traveled home as usual on the bus. He was used to the vile stench of the slaughterhouse, but knew that other people found it stomach-churning and that, as a result, however busy the bus, he would always end up with a double seat to himself. So he didn't notice anything unusual on this particular day, when the other passengers moved seats to get away from him. It wasn't until he reached into his pocket for his cigarettes and put his hands right into the offal that he realized the sick joke. After two years, even Ozzy decided enough was enough and moved on, flitting impatiently from job to job, with periods working as an auto mechanic and a house painter, and a brief two-week stint as a mortuary porter. He even followed his mother to the Lucas electrical plant, where his job was to sit in a soundproofed room all day, tuning new car horns. 'I liked heavy metal better because it was louder,' he later said.

By now the 'Teddy Boy' look was out of fashion and in Birmingham anybody who was anybody was a Mod. Ozzy, now in his late teens, joined in enthusiastically, but it wasn't so much the music – James Brown and other American groups – but the fashions and the fighting that attracted him. Dressed in mohair suits, and shirts with the collars buttoned down, the Mods of the early 1960s made newspaper headlines all over Britain, as they became involved in vicious gang fights with their arch rivals, the Rockers and Teddy Boys. Ozzy wasn't particularly interested in the gang rivalry, he'd never felt especially drawn to one group or another, but the brawls were a different matter. Armed with dustbin lids and iron pokers, Ozzy and his Mod friends would wade in, creating mayhem and havoc wherever they went. Several times Ozzy returned home battered and bleeding, but typically he would give as good as he got. 'I can remember one pitched battle where I deliberately tried to drown some kid. Where I came from, it was kill or be killed. I could be a vicious little fucker,' he recalls. On one occasion, Ozzy went out armed with a set of butcher's meat cleavers. He ended up in a fight with three other youths, but was outnumbered and fell through a glass shop window, seriously cutting his arm. The injury was so severe that he still bears the scar today. Nor was Ozzy's violence simply limited to the streets. Since he was a small child, he had not got on with his brothers, or his sisters Iris and Gillian and, one Sunday, after Iris had thoroughly cleaned the house and banned Ozzy from moving a thing out of place, he flipped, blacking both her eyes.

It was via the Mod scene that Ozzy was first introduced to drugs. He could not have guessed it at the time, but it was to be a love affair that would last almost a quarter of a century, and at times would come close to destroying him. Drugs were as important to most Mods as the music, fashion and violence, and Ozzy jumped in headfirst. Black bombers, dexies, double dex, triple dex, whites, blues. Anything new, anything different, anything illicit and outrageous – Ozzy would try it.

With a growing drug habit to feed, Ozzy needed cash and having just walked out on his job at the car factory – much to the displeasure of his mother, who had persuaded her bosses to give her son a try – he turned to a life of petty crime. While still at school, he had occasionally broken into electricity and gas meters to steal the coins inside and he would also break into the home of his sixty-three-year-old neighbor when she was out at work. For a while, he and a gang of like-minded friends had also enterprisingly run a car-minding service outside their local Aston Villa football ground. Fans would drive to the match and Ozzy and friends would offer to watch their cars throughout the game. Fearful that they would return to a vandalized car if they refused, the supporters would reluctantly hand over the money. The scam only ended when Ozzy decided to expand into offering a cleaning service alongside the minding. His first client returned to find his paintwork destroyed after Ozzy had tried to clean the car with a rough scouring pad. He angrily marched Ozzy home and demanded that John Osbourne Senior make good the damage. Not surprisingly, his father was furious and after paying the bill insisted that the scam stopped there and then.

However, needing to make a living from crime, rather than simply pocket money for records, Ozzy set his sights a little higher. His first target was a clothes shop called Sarah Clarke, for which one of his sisters worked as an agent. The plan was to break in at dead of night and steal as many sweaters as he could carry, and then sell them on at a tidy profit. But Ozzy, being Ozzy, forgot to take a torch and when he emerged from the shop, he found his arms were actually full of piles of children's clothes and women's pantyhose and stockings. Undeterred, he continued with his life of crime, breaking and entering other small shops, a boarding house and private homes. But Ozzy was never destined to be the world's greatest cat burglar. On one occasion he stole a twenty-four inch television set and clambered on to a wall to escape the scene of the crime. He immediately lost his balance and fell off with the television landing right on top of him. He had considered the matter of finger prints, however, and carefully wore a pair of gloves every time he set out; it wasn't until much later that he realized the thumb was missing from one of them and he was actually leaving a perfect set of prints behind at the scene of every crime!

After a while, Ozzy teamed up with another local youth, Pascal Donegal, the son of an Irish drunk. Pascal was kicked out of the house every morning by his dad and, with nothing else to do, fell into bad ways and the company of Ozzy. The dynamic duo decided to target the richer part of town and, after keeping watch on the houses for several days, discovered that one man left the same house at exactly the same time every morning – 7 am. What's more, there didn't seem to be any other sign of life in the house. Ozzy kept watch, while Pascal shimmied up a drainpipe and disappeared inside. The next thing Ozzy saw was Pascal flying out of the bedroom window and crashing down on to the ground in front of him, breaking his leg as he landed. The other occupant of the house, it emerged, worked the night shift and returned home to his bed every day at 6am. He had caught Pascal in his bedroom and literally kicked him out of the window. The door of the house opened and the furious man came out and kicked and punched the helpless Pascal as he lay on the ground. Ozzy fled, leaving Pascal to face the man's fury – and the police – alone. Such an ordeal would have been enough to put off most teenagers, but it took a lot more than that to deter Ozzy.

Convinced that there was still easy money to be made, Ozzy returned to the scene of his first burglary, Sarah Clarke's clothes shop. The local police were wise to him this time and he was arrested as he tried to escape. Charged with Breaking and Entering and Stealing Goods to the value of $36 (£25), Ozzy was found guilty and fined $58 (£40). He clearly didn't have the money to pay the fine and begged his father to help him out. John Osbourne Senior was devoted to his wayward son and thought long and hard, but after much soul-searching eventually told Ozzy that he would not be paying, reasoning that the alternative punishment – a three-month stint in jail – might knock some much-needed sense into his son's head.

To his shock, Ozzy was sent to Winson Green Prison, where he found himself a boy amongst men. As a tearaway teenager in Aston, he was respected, revered and even feared, but here, not quite eighteen, and amongst some of the hardest and most vicious men in Britain, he was out of his depth. Over the next twenty years he would find himself in and out of cells for a variety of crimes, but this was different. He was only a teenager, he had little actual experience of the big, bad world outside his local patch, and his young age and newly grown long hair made him an immediate target of both the prison's gays and hardmen. Terrified that he would find himself on the receiving end of a beating, or sexual abuse at the hands of a frustrated inmate, Ozzy reverted to his old school defense mechanism of clowning around to get himself out of trouble. It worked by and large, but one murderer was so determined to have sex with him, that to escape his advances Ozzy was forced to smash him over the head with one of the huge metal pots used overnight in the cells as toilets. Ozzy served three days in solitary confinement for the offence, but his bravado impressed his fellow inmates and, on his return to the main prison, he became part of the in-crowd, who would torment and bully the prison's sex offenders. Ozzy's justification, now and then, was that the men had been jailed for abusing children and deserved everything they got, and he joined in with relish.

It was during his stay in prison that Ozzy acquired the first of his many tattoos. His grandfather had a tattoo of a snake, which went from his head all the way down to his toes and, as a young boy, Ozzy would sit enthraled for hours, gazing at it. He'd long wanted to copy it, but was too afraid of what his parents might say. Here in jail, with plenty of time on his hands, he set about following in his grandfather's footsteps. His first tattoo – the now world-famous O Z Z Y on the knuckles of his left hand – was done with the aid of a needle and the lead from a pencil. Using the same method, he placed a happy smiling face on each knee, designed to cheer him up when he woke every morning. Before he left jail, he had added the number three to his arm by using a tin of gray polish, which was melted and stuck into the skin with a needle.

After six weeks, Ozzy was released. He was a changed man. His dad had been right. His time in prison had given him a shock and an early lesson that the criminal life simply wasn't worth it. True, there were few opportunities for a young man from his background, with his lack of qualifications and education. But Ozzy now knew that the criminal route was not his way out. Besides, in the three years since he'd first heard 'Love Me Do', The Beatles had gone on to establish themselves as the biggest band in the world. They'd chalked up a further nine number one singles and, although he didn't quite know how he was going to achieve it, Ozzy knew he wanted a taste of the same. His parents had given him everything they could, but he knew he had to move on and leave behind the backstreets of Aston to achieve his dream.

Today Ozzy's millionaire lifestyle – with his palatial homes in Beverly Hills and Buckinghamshire – is a world away from the poverty and drudgery of his formative years. But they were the years that counted; the years that inspired him and helped make the crazy, mixed-up and endlessly fascinating individual that the world loves today. And the bitter-sweet memories of those times still remain with Ozzy today. 'The odd thing is, that wherever I am in the world, in my dreams, whatever I'm being chased by – wild animals, Red Indians, World War Three, whatever – I'll open a door and be back in the house I was born in,' says Ozzy. 'I open the door and I'm in Number 14, Lodge Road, Aston, Birmingham 6.'

chapter two

He's Leaving Home

6 *I discovered rock 'n' roll. You could go round Europe in a van with your best mates, drinking beer, smoking dope and screwing chicks.* 9

OZZY WAS OUT OF JAIL. He was seventeen years old and a free man. He had dreams and ambitions and was determined that somehow he was going to follow them. His taste of prison had put him off a life of crime for good, and his experiences of regular jobs had made him realize that the nine-to-five existence was not for him. 'When I left school I wanted to be a plumber. When I heard The Beatles I wanted to be a singer,' he explained simply. His chance was to come sooner than he expected. Wandering aimlessly around the streets of Aston while half-heartedly looking for a job, he bumped into an old friend who said that he had put together a band called Approach, but was still looking for a singer. Never one to miss a trick, Ozzy declared that he was a singer, and the legend of Ozz was born. His father John, still as devoted as ever to his son, went heavily into debt to give him the money to buy a PA system. The following day, Ozzy dashed down to George Clay's music shop in Birmingham and bought a 50-watt PA system with two mikes. The band rehearsed endlessly in pub rooms, empty cinemas and poky garages, basically anywhere there was a spare room, but they struggled to find anyone who would give them the chance to perform live. Ozzy loved singing and, bowled over by the sound of his own voice amplified for the first time in a microphone, was desperate for others to hear him too. Frustrated, he began to look around for another band that would give him that opportunity. At a club one night he came across Music Machine, who told Ozzy that their regular singer was sick and they needed a stand-in. Ozzy, thrilled by the idea of being able to travel to gigs and meet women, jumped at the chance to fill in. The band played their first gig at the Birmingham Firehouse in front of just three people and followed it with a series of shows at local youth clubs and pubs in the Birmingham area. For Ozzy it was a much longed-for taste of life on the road. He moved out of his parents' house and into an apartment with the other members of the group in a run-down area of Handsworth in Birmingham, but gigs were hard to find and, after a few months of struggling to keep body and soul together, the bandmates agreed to go their separate ways.

With no other source of income, Ozzy made a scant living from buying and selling anything he could lay his hands on. At the same time, he formed another band, Rare Breed, with eighteen-year-old fellow 'Brummie', as those born in Birmingham are known, and bass player Terence Butler, known to his friends as Geezer. Geezer was to remain one of Ozzy's closest friends through thick and thin, but he could never claim that he wasn't warned in those very early days exactly what he was taking on. 'I've seen him take a crap on some guy's car. For no reason. He's crazy. That was two days after I'd met him. He's not mellowed. He's just more subtle now,' he recalled, many years later. Sadly, Rare Breed was to remain just that and after three gigs they too called it a day. But Ozzy would not be put off. Calling himself Ozzy Zig, he placed an advert in his local newspaper and in the window of a music shop in the Bull Ring, the main shopping center in Birmingham, which read: 'Ozzy Zig, vocalist, requires band. Owns own PA.' It was a typically eccentric advert – he'd never been known by that name in his life, but when it popped into his head – from who knows where – Ozzy immediately scribbled it down on to a piece of paper.

Meanwhile, his arch enemy from school, Tony Iommi, had teamed up with an eighteen-year-old truck driver Bill Ward, also from Aston, to form a blues band known as The Rest. Tony played electric guitar and Bill the drums and, after changing their name to Mythology, they moved to Carlisle in Cumbria on the edge of the English Lake District. They gathered a cult following, covering songs by groups such as Cream, The Yardbirds and The Beatles. But they did not make enough to survive, and in the summer of 1968 they disbanded the group and moved back to Birmingham to start all over again. It was there, as they wandered despondently around the center of Birmingham, that they spotted Ozzy's advert. Tony and Bill were already friends with Geezer and went to visit Ozzy in the hope of signing him up. Bill well remembers that fateful day. 'The three of us went over to his house and we knocked on the door and there he was. He had no hair, which kind of turned me off straight away, because I had hair down to my ass. So he said. "Oh, I'll grow my hair out".' But Ozzy's short hair wasn't all they had to contend with. Bizarrely, the singer had opened the front door wearing a long brown robe, with a chimney brush over his shoulder and dragging his shoes along behind him on a dog lead. 'Well, I had to make an impression and I didn't have any money. The brown outfit was my dad's overalls from work,' he said by way of explanation much later. Tony, meanwhile, was dreading the meeting, as he recognized Ozzy's name and was praying it wasn't the same Ozzy that he fought with so viciously at school. However, on meeting, the two teenagers agreed to put their differences behind them in the hope of finally putting together a successful band.

Ozzy chose their name – the Polka Tulk Blues Band, either named after a can of talcum powder sitting in Ozzy's bathroom or after a local Indian clothing store, according to different accounts. They quickly learned eighteen songs and returned to Carlisle to capitalize on Mythology's fan base in the town, soon changing their name to Earth and playing a mixture of jazz and blues. It was not a style that suited them and the band soon began to write their own songs. They were harder and louder than pop and blues with deep, doom-laden mystical lyrics; this 'doom and gloom' music soon became their trademark. Ozzy recalls: 'We got sick and tired of all the bullshit – love your brother and flower-power forever. We're just ordinary backstreet guys and we're just making a sound which is free suburban rock, if you like. Slum rock. The music we developed was loud and it was furious because that's exactly the way we felt at the time.'

It was the sound that would come to be known as heavy metal and would be copied by rock bands the world over. But in the late 60s it still had no name and 'slum rock', as Ozzy dubbed it, was still not to everyone's taste. The band was forced to survive on packed lunches, sandwiches and cigarettes donated by Tony Iommi's mum, who owned a local sweet shop and would occasionally agree to lend them her van. Ozzy was still receiving occasional cash handouts from his mum, but it was still not enough. Ozzy was so broke at this time that he was once forced to walk to rehearsals in bare feet after his last pair of shoes finally collapsed beneath him, and at night he would often break in to people's back gardens to pick and eat raw vegetables straight from the ground. More shockingly, once again, he could not afford underwear. This wasn't a real problem until he developed a hole in his well-worn jeans and ended up giving one audience far more of a show than he had intended.

The band persevered with the usual round of pubs and clubs, waiting for the break that would turn them into the new Beatles, but Ozzy's wild and experimental streak had not left him. His early experiences with speed had given him a taste for drugs and when Bill Ward told him that he could get stoned by smoking banana peel, Ozzy couldn't wait to try. The group bought a huge bunch of bananas, ate them and then put the peel under the grill of the oven to dry them out ready to smoke. The four teenagers ended up fleeing the premises after setting the kitchen on fire, but once the smoke had subsided they returned – as determined as ever – to scrape together the burnt remains of the banana skins and roll them into joints.

Over the following year, Earth were to establish themselves as a solid support act, opening for bands such as Jethro Tull. The bat-biting episode was more than a decade away, but even then Ozzy was proving himself an outrageous showman, prepared to go to any lengths to captivate his audience. At one particular gig, he noticed to his frustration that the audience were chatting amongst themselves during their set as they waited for the main headline band to appear. Irritated by this, he disappeared backstage, coated his face, hands and feet in purple paint and returned to the stage, screaming at the audience to shut up and listen. The purple paint proved a one-off, but Ozzy's determination to grab an audience's attention and hold on to it until he decided otherwise was to remain with him. By 1969 Earth were on their last legs and after bombing at a disastrous show in their hometown – it emerged that the audience had been expecting a tuxedo-clad dance band by the same name – they decided to drop the name and search for something a little more suitable. The four young men may have looked and dressed like hippies, but the similarities ended there; they wanted a name and an image that suited their rough heavy backstreet sound and they did not have to wait long for inspiration.

The band rehearsed in an old garage across the road from a cinema and Ozzy commented one day how it was strange that people were prepared to pay good money to be terrified by a horror film. Perhaps people would pay good money, too, to be scared by a rock band? The group chose the deliberately sinister-sounding name Black Sabbath, based on a 1935 Boris Karloff movie, their favorite horror film. 'It was just a different angle. At the time it was all bells and flowers, hippies and incense and smoking hash,' Ozzy recalled. At the same time, while rehearsing new material, the band underwent a strange supernatural experience. Geezer and Tony were independently trying out some new riffs for Ozzy and Bill, when all of a sudden they played exactly the same notes at the same speed at the same time. This had never happened before. Convinced it was an omen, the band agreed to name the song Black Sabbath, too.

It was during this period that the band first began to wear the trademark crucifixes that Ozzy – more than thirty years later – is still never seen without. The crucifixes came about after all four members of the band had the same dream during the space of a week. Initially everyone kept quiet, but late one night in the van Ozzy told the others what he had dreamt. Bill Ward recalls: 'I just went "Holy fucking shit! The same fucking dream!" Then everyone joined in and everybody admitted it. We had a visitation.' By coincidence, Ozzy's father John had made four aluminum crosses at work for the band to wear. Bill says: 'He recognized that there was something going on here that possibly he couldn't understand, but he was possibly seeing Ozz doing something real for the first time in his life and so he made four crosses. It was almost like a reaction from Ozz's father to say, "Hey, you take care of big Ozz".'

During their time as Earth the band had played at a local Birmingham venue called Henry's Blueshouse. The local promoter who booked them was Jim Simpson. Impressed by their raw talent, he persuaded the newly formed Black Sabbath that he should be their manager and succeeded in getting them their first London gig, at the famous Marquee Club in Soho. The London club had never seen anything like it. The band performed in brightly colored pajama jackets and Ozzy walked around the stage with a hot water faucet on a piece of string tied around his neck. The wild man of Birmingham, already gathering a following in his hometown, went down a storm, but heard nothing more after returning to Birmingham and eventually contacted the manager of the club to find out why. The manager told them frankly that he didn't mind giving them another gig, but next time would they mind having a bath before they arrived.

Within months the band had been booked to play the Star Club in Hamburg, Germany. For Ozzy it was the high spot of his life. He still worshipped The Beatles – their mid to late 60s albums – *Revolver, Rubber Soul, Sergeant Pepper's Lonely Hearts Club Band* and the *White Album* – remain amongst his favorite records today, and throughout his career he has always insisted on listening to Beatles' music before he goes on stage. The Star Club was where The Beatles had got their first break six years earlier. Black Sabbath had broken their record at the club for the longest-held house attendance and Ozzy knew this meant the big time.

It was during their stint in Germany that Ozzy created the famous ear-busting rock volume that was to go on to be the trademark of heavy metal music. Chattering audiences had annoyed him back in Britain; this time round he simply wasn't going to put up with it. 'So we used to play really loud,' Ozzy explains, 'as loud as we could get it, trying to drown out all conversation in the club.' Every other heavy rock act began to copy them and bands became so loud that, in the north of England, Leeds City Council introduced a 'ninety-six decibel law'. If any band's volume rose above that level the amplifiers would cut out. Ozzy naturally didn't consider his night's work complete unless they were cut off at least three times.

Shortly after their return from Germany, the band were asked to record a cover of Crow's 'Evil Woman (Don't Play Your Games With Me)' as their first single and, although it made little impression, it did help them earn their first recording contract with Vertigo Records. Their first album, entitled *Black Sabbath*, was recorded in twelve hours, spread over three days, for just $870 (£600) on an eight-track machine at Regent Sound in London. Ozzy's beloved Beatles had recorded their *Sergeant Pepper* album on a four-track machine and created one of the most memorable albums of all time. If simplicity was good enough for them, it was good enough for Black Sabbath, Ozzy reasoned. It was released, fittingly, on Friday 13 February 1970. By the following month, it had reached Number Twenty-Three in the American Album charts and Number Eight in Britain, sharing the Top Ten with The Beatles, The Who, Simon & Garfunkel and Andy Williams. Ozzy and Black Sabbath had arrived.

Ozzy, however, was happy just to be able to show his mother that his voice was finally recorded on a piece of vinyl. 'I remember when the first single came out. We were still grubbing around playing any shithole we could get booked into and my mother was still screaming at me to get a proper job,' Ozzy recalls. Now he had a proper job and he was determined to pay his mother back for all the handouts that had kept him going since his time in jail. With the $72.50 (£50) that each band member had received for the album, Ozzy bought himself a decent pair of shoes and his first bottle of Brut aftershave, and then went back to 14 Lodge Road, where he proudly handed the rest of the money over to his tearful but proud mother. Remembering the happy family singsongs of a few years earlier, she pulled up a chair and Ozzy's first record was proudly placed on the turntable of the family Dansette record player. His dad opened a bottle of beer to lubricate his throat in anticipation, but from the first track – a dark, doom-laden version of the title song 'Black Sabbath' which opened with the sound of a tolling church bell and rainfall – it was clear that this was no jolly sing-along record. His mum and dad sat in bemused silence with fixed smiles, and listened patiently as track after indecipherable track blasted their eardrums. Ozzy, desperate for their approval, asked afterwards whether they had enjoyed it. While his mum made her excuses and headed to the kitchen for a headache tablet, his dad nodded and reassured him that he was sure it would go down well with young people, although he couldn't help adding: 'Are you sure you were just drinking alcohol? This isn't music, this is weird.'

Throughout his childhood, Ozzy had gone out on a limb and aged twenty-two he was no different; he was still making waves. The band's record company had chosen to place an upside down cross on the gatefold of the album and controversy erupted when the album hit the shops. The band's dark image attracted weirdos in their thousands, and very quickly the crosses made for the group by Ozzy's father were to come in handy. As Ozzy and Sabbath toured Europe and America promoting the album, they were approached by a satanic cult asking them to perform at their 'Night of Satan' festival to be held at Stonehenge in England. They declined and were immediately threatened with an evil spell. By now they were already attached to their crosses and always wore them on stage, but vowed from then on to wear them twenty-four hours a day. Few of the songs that Ozzy belted out on stage every night actually dealt with anything truly satanic, but their reputation now went before them. Before one concert in Memphis, Tennessee, the band's dressing rooms were covered in crosses drawn with animal blood. During the same show, a Satanist tried to stab Tony on stage, claiming that he would sacrifice the guitarist's soul to the Devil, and after the show a coven of witches waited outside the band's hotel in the hope of being saved by them. Terrified of being killed in the crush, Geezer chanted a fake spell to clear the crowd. Bill Ward recalls: 'Some people would say "God, we were really frightened to meet you, and we're quite surprised, now we've met you. It's not like the way we thought." I think Ozzy felt the same way about it. I mean, yes, we liked the idea of what's beyond, but as an interest. Certainly in no way as the practise of such.' As Ozzy himself says: 'We didn't plan it. We tried to put music over in a different angle. It had an evil sound, a heavy doom sound. And then there were all these fucking witches and freaks phoning us, wanting us to play at black masses and all this crap.'

But while Ozzy claimed to have no real interest in the occult, the occult seemed to be developing a strange interest in him. Maybe it was the drugs, but inexplicable things were beginning to happen, and not for the last time, Ozzy began to wonder if he was losing his mind. In 1973, to record their fifth album *Sabbath Bloody Sabbath*, the band hired a castle in Wales. It was a remote, scary place and one day, as Ozzy and Tony walked from the rehearsal room towards the armory, where the castle's weapons and armor were stored, they saw a man dressed from head to foot in black walking towards them. He disappeared through a side door into another room, but when Ozzy followed him there was nobody there. 'It was creepy, really creepy,' recalls Tony. The castle's owners later told them that the place was haunted and that they had clearly seen a ghost. A few weeks later came another, more serious incident. After a late night recording, Ozzy had fallen asleep by the fireside. As he slumbered, his blankets caught fire.

He was saved only when Tony and Geezer smelt the smoke from another room and rushed in to drag him clear of the flames. The band was seriously disturbed by their experiences. So disturbed that, although *Sabbath Bloody Sabbath* was one of the most critically acclaimed albums of their entire career, Ozzy insisted that it was time for them to cut their ties with the occult once and for all.

The band by now had taken America by storm. They made their first appearance in the States in New York, in October 1970. They were the first heavy rock band to play the US, and America had never seen anything like it before. Neither had Ozzy. 'Touring America in the early seventies as a big success meant we had people throwing drugs at us all the time,' he remembers. 'It was all "Toot this, man!" and "Stick this one up your ass, man!"'

The flamboyant lead singer was beginning to attract his fair share of women, too. Growing up as a typical teenager in working-class Birmingham, Ozzy, like most of his friends, had struggled to attract girls. Pre-Pill and pre-sexual liberation, there were few opportunities for a gawky, yet red-blooded, sexually frustrated teenager. 'I was never good with girls when I was younger,' Ozzy later admitted. 'I didn't know what to do, so I would get drunk and when I finally decided to make my move I'd get up and fall flat on my face on the table.'

In America, Ozzy was able to make up for lost time; the girls couldn't care less whether he was drunk or sober, standing up or falling down, and he lapped it up like a kid in a candy store. 'We worked our asses off and things got a bit crazy really,' he remembers. 'The groupies, the pills, all that shit was starting to happen for us and things were getting wild. The groupies knew more about our tour itineraries than we did and we suffered the results as well.' Soon Ozzy and the boys were gold card members at their local VD clinic, being

47

treated for every sexually transmitted disease under the sun and a few that still hadn't yet been discovered. For a change, penicillin rather than cocaine was their drug of choice. 'We got clap, crabs, all sorts of exotic diseases. And then we'd have to go through the cures, which were generally worse.'

These were the carefree days of sexual freedom, pre-AIDS and long before monogamy became fashionable. Ozzy was a notch on every self-respecting groupie's bedpost and he didn't mind one bit. In fact, for a young man in his early twenties, who had left Birmingham virtually a virgin, he couldn't believe his luck. Relationships didn't come into it. Never mind knowing the girls' surnames, Ozzy rarely ever got to know their first names.

'Towards the end I started wondering why I bothered,' Ozzy recalls. 'At least in Britain there was a challenge, but with groupies there was no challenge at all. It was meet her, have a drink, get her stoned, fuck her and then push her out the back door.' On one occasion in West Virginia a groupie turned up at Ozzy's hotel room looking for sex. He obliged and a few minutes after she left there was a knock on the door. 'I think she's forgotten something, but it's a different chick at the door. Beautiful as fucking God,' recalls Ozzy. Ozzy couldn't resist and ended up sleeping with her too, but a few minutes after she left there was another knock at the door. This went on until an exhausted Ozzy locked his door on the fifth and final groupie of the night.

It was a testament to his stamina that there was anything left to put into making records. But the cult of Sabbath and heavy metal had well and truly kicked in and Ozzy was determined to work his socks off to hang on to it, churning out album after album. A second record, *Paranoid*, which gave them a British Number Four hit in September 1970 with the single of the same

Almost respectable: Ozzy – flanked by Marilyn Manson and Robbie Williams – is immortalized on the Hollywood Walk of Fame, April 2002

© Sara De Boer / Retna Limited, USA

Besides three children by Sharon, Ozzy fathered a daughter and son by his first wife, Thelma, as well as adopting her son by a previous marriage. With their son Louis in 1981 *mirrorpix.com*

With Sharon at the première of *Little Nicky*
at Mann's Chinese Theater, Hollywood, in 2000.
Ozzy played himself in the movie
© *Steve Granitz / Retna Limited, USA*

Eighteen-year-old Aimee with her mother at the Hollywood Walk of Fame ceremony, April 2002

© Sara De Boer/Retna Ltd, USA

Live at Ozzfest in June 2001, aged fifty-two – still turning in electrifying performances
© Hayley Madden / Redferns

Ozzy is transformed *(left)* for the cover shot of his album *Bark at the Moon* (December 1983); with his daughter Aimee, aged three weeks *(right)*

Ken Lennox

Main: Performing with Zakk Wylde, whom Ozzy recruited from a New Jersey bar in 1988
© Tony Mottram/Retna

Inset: More black humor than Black Sabbath: perhaps the cross is to ward off photographers
© AKI/Retna

A Star Is Born – Ozzy surrounded by family and friends on Hollywood Boulevard, a month after *The Osbournes* began transmission in the US © *Sara De Boer / Retna Limited, USA*

The original
members of Black
Sabbath, reunited
thirty years on
© Mick Hutson /
Redferns

Well, any
ageing rock star
might be a little
hard of hearing –
but what about
the third hand?
Lars Sjogren /
FAMOUS

A bemused-looking Ozzy giving
a passable impression of
the Cat in the Hat
© *Capital Pictures*

name, followed. The album reached Number One in Britain and Number Twelve in the US charts, going on to sell over four million copies. A third album, *Master of Reality* was recorded the following year. It went to Number Five in the UK and Number Eight in America, reaching platinum status shortly afterwards. In 1972 came *Black Sabbath Volume 4*, which reached Number Eight in the UK charts and Number Thirteen in the States. A year later came the acclaimed *Sabbath Bloody Sabbath*, a Number Four hit in the UK and Number Eleven in the US, which had sold more than a million copies within its first year of release. The 1975 release of *Sabotage*, became a Number Seven hit in the UK album charts and reached Number Twenty-Eight in America.

Critics still detested them, along with parents and hippies. But teenagers could not get enough of them and their profile had now grown to such an extent that they could sell out respectable venues, such as London's Royal Albert Hall and New York's Madison Square Garden. Heavy rock was now a growing phenomenon in both Britain and America. There'd been Elvis, rock and roll, The Beatles and flower power, but the screech and crash of metal music was something new, and the unique sound that Sabbath had created had been copied by dozens of other bands. Led Zeppelin, Deep Purple and a host of wannabes were aping the long hair, black clothes, screeching guitars, lyrics reveling in black magic and fantasy and mammoth guitar riffs.

But what the other bands could not replicate was a lead singer like Ozzy. In Ozzy, Black Sabbath had a true working-class hero and one of the most dynamic front men of his era. With his flat, almost tuneless, banshee wail and his contorted face, he would jump, scream, swear, snarl and race up and down the stage. Dressed in white catsuits and with a mane of long brown hair, he was uncontrollable and unpredictable and the wilder he got, the more audiences loved him. He invented head-banging – the traditional heavy metal dance where the audience shakes its head violently in time to the music. It wasn't a cynical marketing exercise – it was merely Ozzy letting off steam in his inimitable way. He also began diving into the audience onto a sea of waving hands, to be passed round by the frenzied crowd before security jumped in to rescue him. Audiences had never seen anything like it and they wanted more, more, more.

Ozzy couldn't believe it. He had started out wanting to be as big as The Beatles, but now The Beatles had split up and he was the rock star the whole word was taking about. It's a rock and roll cliché that a singer should squander his new-found wealth on sex, drugs, loose women and fast cars. But if the word excess covered the behavior of those who had gone before him, it wasn't sufficient to span the exploits of a man who simply didn't understand the meaning of the word 'No'. 'We got success and we thought we were the kings of the fucking earth,' Ozzy says. 'Two years before, if someone had said, "You can have this white powder for a hundred quid", we would have said: "Fuck you, man. A hundred quid? You must be joking". My old man never saw a hundred quid all his life you know. It's just spoils of war, if you like. It's what you go through.'

Ozzy treated himself to a huge farm in Staffordshire that he filled with jukeboxes and pinball machines. He started collecting shotguns and air rifles, and so many flash cars clogged his driveway that he once smashed up a V12 Jaguar simply to make way for another car he was having delivered the following day. But it was drugs, rather than fast cars, that were Ozzy's real weakness. Everyone in the band was drinking and taking as much hash, Quaaludes and LSD as they could lay their hands on. But Ozzy outdid them all. And his favorite was the drug that was to be his personal crutch and torment for many years to come – cocaine. 'We were very heavily involved with cocaine for a while,' he recalls. 'Actually, we were heavily involved in everything. Every single day we were touring we got completely out of our fucking minds. Coke, dope, acid, more coke, alcohol, always alcohol. We never stopped! In my whole life I think I've probably taken about 900 acid tabs and they were all taken during those years. I used to swallow handfuls at a time.' At his worst, Ozzy took seven different drugs on one day. 'I don't suggest that anyone tries this,' he said afterwards. 'It took me about eight days to feel normal again. I was a fucking nutter.' By the time of the recording of *Volume 4*, Ozzy's drug habit had become so bad that he would sit in the Jacuzzi all day, snorting cocaine. Every so often, when called, he would get up and record a new song, before diving back in to the bubbles for another line. The band were getting through so much of the stuff that it was delivered to them in soap powder boxes. Ozzy desperately wanted to call the album *Snowblind* as a tribute, but the record company refused, and instead he had to make do with a credit on the album sleeve, which read: 'Thanks to the COKE-Cola Company'.

Ozzy had always prided himself on never appearing on stage drunk. He admitted that he would often be carrying hangovers from the previous day at eight o'clock at night, but he would never have actually taken a drink before he stepped on stage. Coke, however, was a different ball game entirely. Ozzy had always suffered from stage fright and by now he was snorting several lines before a show. At the 1974 California Jam in Ontario, California – one of the biggest gigs of their career – the band were helicoptered to the site, where seconds before going on stage to face an audience of more than 400,000, Tony brought out a five-inch high vial and shook out the contents on to a table. Ozzy's cocaine use was matched only by his drinking. Once, in Memphis, Tennessee, Ozzy woke to find himself lying in the middle of a busy freeway with cars racing past him on either side. So drunk that he was barely able to walk, he staggered over to a nearby parked car to relieve himself. Unfortunately, Ozzy had chosen a parked-up police car and promptly found himself arrested. 'This lady cop went apeshit watching this drunken limey pissing on her wheel!' While Ozzy lapped up all the cocaine and booze he could lay his hands on, he chose to stay clear of heroin. 'Don't get me wrong – we tried it a few times, but all it did for me was make me violently sick. You have to really want to get in to that drug, it's like a fulltime job and I just couldn't be bothered with it.' It was all Ozzy could do to hold down the job he had, let alone taking on the job of yet another drug. The endless touring and recording, combined with a lack of sleep and his growing alcohol and drugs intake, were taking their toll, and by 1975 Ozzy was teetering on the brink. As the band got bigger and bigger, the records took longer to record, with that year's album *Sabotage* taking a full year to make. If the album had cost $72,500 (£50,000) to record, then double that was spent on coke. While all the band were in it up to their eyeballs, Ozzy was snorting the stuff like it was going out of fashion. He was out of control – not for the first time and certainly not for the last – and desperately needed a break. One of the album's tracks 'Am I Going Insane?' appeared as a single that year and summed up the desperate state he now found himself in. 'I used to think I was never going home again,' he recalls. 'And that combined with all the parties we had after gigs and all the assholes that used to hang around us really started getting to me in a bad way. For me, everything went downhill from there. It was beginning to drive me nuts.'

chapter three

Mad, Bad and Dangerous?

> ❝ *I am something of a madman. I can do nothing in moderation. If it's booze, I drink the place dry. If it's drugs, I take everything and then scrape the carpet for little crumbs.* ❞

OZZY WAS SHATTERED. Five years of back-to-back tours and recording sessions, fuelled only by drink and drugs, had drained every last drop of physical and mental energy he had left. He had dreamt of nothing but home for months and now to his immense relief he was finally there. During his time on the road, he had met and somehow found time to marry a local girl back home in Birmingham. Thelma Mayfair had caught his eye and, after a whirlwind romance, the couple had married in 1971. Thelma already had a son from a previous marriage, a boy by the name of Elliot Kingsley, who was five years old when they married; Ozzy decided to adopt the boy. They had gone on to have two children of their own – the suitably showbusiness-named Jessica Starshine, born in 1972, and a son Louis, born in 1975.

Ozzy was devoted to his kids and missed them terribly when he was away. He and Thelma had experienced their ups and downs, caused mainly by his long absences on the road, but they had stuck it out, and what Ozzy needed now he was home was to bury himself in the bosom of his family and get to know his kids again. No more concerts, no more twenty-four hoursessions in the studio. No more riotous parties or drugs. Just some quiet time on his farm and a little tender, loving care. Someone to snuggle up under the duvet with him, bring him a cup of tea and then leave him undisturbed for three weeks while he slept off the world's biggest ever hangover. The limo was dropping him off at his door and all he had to do was walk inside and it would all be behind him.

Things did not go quite according to plan, however. The first thing Ozzy saw on walking through the door was a letter on the doormat. He opened it, and to his horror, discovered that he was expected back in the recording studio the following Monday. He hadn't been warned that this was even a remote possibility and he flipped. Ozzy had little patience at the best of times and, strung out from months on the road, he just couldn't cope. As the red mist descended, he flung his bags hard against the wall, ran in to the kitchen and grabbed his shotgun. At the same time, Thelma, unaware of quite how fragile a state her husband had returned in, called down the stairs. She'd be down in a second to say hello and make him a cup of tea, but in the meantime could he possibly help her out by feeding the chickens in the yard. It was the final straw. 'When she said that, I thought "I'll feed them all right. I'll feed them a half a ton of lead!"' Ozzy recalls. 'So I went down to the bottom of the yard where they were standing. I took a box of cartridges and my shotgun and I blasted the hell out of them all. There was blood and feathers everywhere . . . poor fuckers didn't know what hit them!'

Ozzy's neighbor, a well-to-do woman, rushed out into her garden to see what the noise was all about. The sight that met her would have had most sensible people running for cover, but having had previous brushes with her crazy rock star neighbor, she knew that where Ozzy was concerned you should always expect the unexpected. She wasn't to be disappointed, for having blown all but one of the chickens away with the shotgun, Ozzy was now maniacally chasing the sole survivor around the yard with a saber. When Ozzy clapped eyes on his neighbor he stopped in his tracks, panting from his exertions, with a wild look in his eyes. 'So I'm standing there with this smoking gun under my arm, knee-deep in dead chickens, and she just looked at me and said, "Unwinding, John?"' he recalls. 'I nearly had fuck-ing hysterics.'

By rights Ozzy should have been the happiest man on the planet. Black Sabbath's 1975 tour had been greeted with unprecedented hysteria. Groups such as Deep Purple and Led Zeppelin were beginning to change their direction, leaving the traditional heavy rock ground almost exclusively to them. But the pressure of life at the top was getting to him.

There were now almost daily wrangles with Tony Iommi, ostensibly about the direction of the band, but, in reality, power struggles about whose band it actually was. Unbelievably, Tony was demanding that he occupy the center stage spot when they performed live, relegating Ozzy to one side. In an interview after the band split up, Ozzy recalled: 'That wasn't my decision and I wasn't very happy – being made to perform at side of stage.'

The band's legal problems were also beginning to get to him, too. Sabbath had parted company with original manager Jim Simpson in September 1970. A new management team of Patrick Meehan and Wilf Pine had persuaded the band that Simpson was mismanaging them and that they would be better off with them. Simpson had later gone on to accuse Sabbath of wrongfully terminating his contract, but at the same time the band had discovered that they had missed out on millions of dollars in potential royalties. To their shock the band lost a lengthy court battle with Simpson and found themselves forced to pay him a large percentage of what little royalties remained. Giving away half their fortune when they had already blown the other half on wild living was a shock to them all, particularly Ozzy, who had spent his share of the money like it was going out of fashion.

To make matters worse, things were starting to go wrong with their new managers, too. Patrick Meehan had originally toured with the band when he first took over their management, but with Black Sabbath's increasing success, he began to spend more and more time at his office. Ozzy felt that Patrick was living it up back at home while they were on the road doing all the hard work, and relations grew increasingly strained. In 1976 Sabbath parted company with Meehan and Pine and, after a brief attempt at looking after themselves, agreed to bring in another new manager by the name of Don Arden. Arden, who hailed from Manchester in England, was the President of Jet Records. He had made a success of managing bands such as The Move and The Small Faces and was now looking after the Electric Light Orchestra who were huge stars in mid-1970s Britain. He was the Mr Big of the pop world and Ozzy and the band thought he was just the man to guide their careers to the next level. It was at this time that twenty-seven year-old Ozzy first met the woman who would become his second wife. Sharon Arden was Don's young daughter and she worked as her father's receptionist. Her first introduction to Ozzy was when he walked into their offices wearing a faucet around his neck. After being introduced to the timid teenager, Ozzy promptly sat down on the floor, refusing to use a chair. Sharon, not surprisingly, was terrified and even asked another secretary to take Ozzy a cup of tea, rather than have to encounter him again.

After signing up with Don, Ozzy and the band relocated to America to escape Britain's tax laws. They released a compilation album *We Sold Our Soul for Rock 'n' Roll*, which was quickly followed by their seventh album, *Technical Ecstasy*, recorded in the States. But Ozzy was starting to grow adrift from his band-mates and – becoming more and more dependent on drugs and drink – was finding it harder and harder to maintain his enthusiasm. He says: 'The last Sabbath albums were very depressing for me. I was doing it for the sake of what we could get off the record company and just get fat on beer and put a record out. Nobody was really interested in promoting it. No one was interested in getting out there and working on the road.'

One of the problems was that Ozzy, easily bored at the best of times, was irritated that each new album seemed to be taking longer to make than the last. Tony Iommi had become the band's official producer on *Technical Ecstasy* – 'the biggest mistake we ever made in my opinion,' recalls Ozzy. Tony took his job extremely seriously and would labor for hours over every chord and every lyric. It was to make for what he felt was a technically perfect album, but to Ozzy the final recording missed the hard, rough edge of their previous releases. 'I think people like to hear the guitar player make a slight mistake, so it sounds like a human being playing instead of a robot,' he said. What's more, Ozzy was concerned that an album heavily reliant on studio wizardry would be almost impossible to replicate live on stage. When it was released, it was to a mixed reception: the album's sound wasn't considered heavy enough by many hardcore fans and critics challenged their change of direction. Ozzy was bitter; he felt he had warned the others that it wouldn't work and, when the band set off on a promotional tour of America in 1977 to support the album, relations between Ozzy and the other three members of Sabbath declined even further.

Tony's pursuit of artistic excellence was by now extending to his stage performances. What had kept Ozzy going through the interminable hours in the recording studio was the thought of the buzz of live performance again. But on stage he found Tony would take lengthy breaks between songs to ensure his guitar was perfectly tuned. 'Sometimes it felt like it took him twenty-five minutes to tune the bloody thing between numbers. And half a minute can lose you an audience if you're not careful. They've paid to hear music, not listen to silence,' said Ozzy bitterly. Tony was also starting to indulge himself with his guitar solos. Guitar solos have long been a key ingredient in any live show, particularly in heavy metal, but Ozzy felt they were getting too long. And if they were boring him then surely, he reasoned, they would be boring the audience, too. 'I used to walk off stage and have a cigarette at first, then I found I had time for a couple of beers and a cigarette. In the end I could have gone across the road for a three-course meal and still got back in time for the next verse,' he recalls.

The only way Ozzy could unwind was to let off steam, as only he knew how. On one occasion, while the band waited for a plane at an airport, he crept up on an unsuspecting stranger and set fire to his newspaper while he was reading it. On another, confined to bed with a sore throat by the tour doctor and ordered to stay off drink, he set off the sprinklers in his room by holding a lit box of matches directly under the fire sensor. The fire brigade were called and the entire hotel had to be evacuated. 'They were all at this gold disk presentation party down the hall and I'd got to go to bed early and I was bored stiff,' he said later, by way of explanation. And that was Ozzy sober. In drink, he was even wilder. 'As soon as we got on the bus after the show, I'd be drinking four bottles of Hennessey a night and cases of beer. I had a coke habit and I smoked like a train,' Ozzy recalls. 'But this is the only job where the more messed up you get, the more they like you. If you turn up at your office job full of heroin, they say "Sorry, mate, you're fired."' To amuse himself, he would creep up on the tour roadies and shave their eyebrows off while they slept, and once, in a hotel lobby, he decided he couldn't wait to find a toilet and squatted in the corner to relieve himself. When the indignant manager roared up, Ozzy responded: 'It's alright mate, I'm a resident.'

Ozzy acknowledged later, 'I always seemed to end up in trouble, it's the story of my life. I remember going to get a prescription for a headache pill and suddenly the drugs squad invade the chemist and I'm whipped off somewhere. If there's a crowd of people, the finger is always pointed at me, so therefore I give them what they want. I'll throw a pie at somebody's head or I'll throw some cat through a window – I don't give a damn, because I'm me. I can't change. I've sat down at times and thought, "It's about time you started to get normal," but what's normal?' The other band members by now were used to Ozzy's wild ways, but even they could not see the funny side when they caught Ozzy ripping up the Gideon Bibles that had been placed in their hotel rooms. After their strange experiences of the supernatural while recording *Sabbath Bloody Sabbath*, the band now erred on the side of caution when it came to anything to do with religion. Not surprisingly a furious row broke out, which ended with Tony punching Ozzy on the nose.

Ozzy turned increasingly to drugs and drink, but these props couldn't mask the underlining problems that were troubling him. From as far back as 1971, he had suffered on and off from depression caused by the grinding monotony of life on the road, and things were now getting worse. 'When I'm on tour in the States I'll stop to call home and they'll say "Where are you?" and I say "I don't know," and nobody believes me,' Ozzy explained at the time. 'But it's true, you get completely disorientated and it does terrible things to your mind.' The depression, he believed, also had a genetic link. 'My whole family's fucking nuts,' he once said bluntly. My whole family has this fucking thing of lunacy, you know?' By his own admission, Ozzy was certainly highly strung. Doctors had periodically given him drugs to help control his condition, but Ozzy simply mixed them in to the cocktail he was already taking.

The American tour was immediately followed by a British tour. When he could, Ozzy would go home for the night in the hope that it would help him calm down, but it did little good and, one night, his frightened wife Thelma ended up taking him to a mental hospital after finding him driving his sports car round and round a small field the whole night long. He refused to stay and returned to the tour, but when it ended in November 1977, Ozzy was a pathetic sight. He suffered from blackouts and, too drugged or drunk to think straight, he was devastated when the rest of the band told him that they were already in the process of booking a recording studio to begin work on yet another album. It was the final straw and Ozzy broke down in tears. He already felt that he was spending too much time away from his wife and children – the only stable force in his life. It was too much, and Ozzy announced to the band that he could no longer cope. He quit and, after a brief press conference in which he pointedly told the press he intended to pursue a solo career of 'good basic hard rock', he returned to his farm in Staffordshire. His marriage to Thelma was now only hanging together by a thread and Ozzy finally realized he needed help. 'My day consisted of getting up, getting myself a drink as soon as possible, going straight down the pub at opening time, staying there all day, and taking more and more coke to keep me going,' he recalls. 'Eventually I was in a terrible state; I couldn't eat, I couldn't sleep, I couldn't even control my own body – nothing. That's when I decided I was definitely going fucking mad.' The end came when, after a day of heavy drug taking, he came home and shot the family cats. 'We had about seventeen and I went crazy and shot them all. My wife found me under the piano in a white suit holding a shotgun in one hand and a knife in the other.' The chickens clearly hadn't been a one-off, and in desperation Ozzy checked himself into a mental hospital. 'If I was going to go completely, uncontrollably crazy I figured I'd better get some professional help,' he says. His stay however was to be a short one. 'Eventually the doctor came in and the first thing he asked me was how often do I masturbate?' Ozzy recalls. 'I turned to this guy and I says, "Listen, asshole, I'm here for my head, not my cock." I was out of there like a shot, running home, desperate for another line.'

After Ozzy left, Black Sabbath struggled to find a suitable replacement and in January 1978, although he clearly still had problems, they persuaded him to return to record their eighth album *Never Say Die*. It was to end up costing them $500,000 (£345,000) to make, their most expensive album to date. In Ozzy's absence, the band had hired Dave Walker, formerly of Fleetwood Mac, to write material for the new album, but when Ozzy returned he refused to sing a single song that had been written by Walker, and the band were forced to rip everything up and rewrite it all. It was not the best of starts. To make matters worse, they found themselves holed up in Toronto, Ontario for five months in the middle of winter. It was Tony's choice of venue; he'd picked the studio because the Rolling Stones had recorded one of their albums there, but it didn't go down well with Ozzy. Canadian winters are only for the very hardy, and for a heavy metal singer used to living in T-shirts and thin denim jackets, it was a miserable time. For a while Ozzy had felt that Tony set too much store by the actual location of the studio. He complained that Tony was wasting far too much time trekking from country to country, house to house, looking for the perfect place for them to work. Canada was the final straw. In his view, you'd either got it or you hadn't and it shouldn't really matter that much where you recorded. After all, the band had started life rehearsing in a poky backstreet Birmingham garage. It had worked for them then, so why did they need anywhere fancier now? The band were conscious that the studio was costing them a fortune and felt they couldn't waste a single second, so with no songs to start work on, they agreed to write in the morning, rehearse in the afternoon and record in the evening. When it did work, Ozzy complained that it felt like a conveyor belt, but more often than not, they would fall behind on the schedule. Bill Ward was by now drinking heavily, while Ozzy and Geezer were mixing drink with copious amounts of dope. Frequently it was left to Tony to try to keep the album together. 'They'd all walk down to the pub and leave me in the rehearsal room trying to come up with a riff,' he complained afterwards. 'Then they'd come back two hours later and say "Got anything?" They thought of me as a machine. And they'd say, "Oh, right, okay. Well, we're going to bed now. We'll try it tomorrow." They were too drunk, man.'

Even when the songs were completed, Ozzy found to his frustration that Tony had established a similar studio set-up to the one that had so frustrated him during the recording of *Technical Ecstasy*. There were more overdubs, yet more use of studio sound and, when a band of thirty trumpeters turned up in the studio early one Sunday morning to play on one of the tracks, Ozzy was outraged. 'It nearly made my hair fall out,' he recalls. 'I was expecting Billy Smart's Circus to turn up offering to manage us.' He complained bitterly to Tony, but found to his disappointment that Geezer and Bill wouldn't rock the boat and would tend to go along with whatever Tony suggested. More and more, he was beginning to feel the outsider of the band.

In June of the same year the single 'Never Say Die' saw the group on *Top of the Pops* and back in the British Top Thirty singles chart for the first time since 'Paranoid'. It was a surprise success, as well as a rebuff to the punks who now dominated the charts, and had written off groups such as Sabbath as obsolete dinosaurs. But, despite the triumph, Ozzy was still unhappy. He felt the band were living off their name, knowing that on one tour alone they could make enough money to live for a whole year. He felt the band had completely lost their direction and, in a heated exchange in the recording studio, he told Tony exactly what he thought. Ozzy accused Tony of becoming heavy metal's answer to Frank Sinatra and complained that the new album was too light and poppy for Black Sabbath's hard-core fans.

The band predictably went back on the road again on what they called their Tenth Anniversary Tour, but it was clear Ozzy's heart was not in it. A concert in Nashville, Tennessee had to be cancelled suddenly when the singer simply didn't show up. (He'd fallen asleep in the wrong hotel room and nobody had been able to find him.) Furious fans did $40,000 (£27,580) of damage to the stadium. 'And the FBI thought I'd been kidnapped and circulated a picture of me to every bar in Nashville,' recalls Ozzy with a chuckle. But at that time, the laughs were becoming few and far between. Tours had previously been a time to let off steam and have fun – a chance to bond again over drink and drugs and girls – but this time round there was a frosty atmosphere. Up-and-coming metal band Van Halen were opening for Black Sabbath, and the new band's enthusiasm and sense of fun made Ozzy realize just what he was missing. With no management to fight with, the band had turned in on itself and there would be constant bickering and quarrels over everything from money to the stage set. 'When you consider that you live together in a confined area for months on end, it helps if you can have a little bit of fun and let off steam, like throw a bottle at somebody,' Ozzy explained. 'We'd come off stage and go our own ways. It was like, he'd go to his room, I'd go to this bar, somebody would go to a strip club. It's an unhealthy situation to be in.'

Ozzy also felt that the rest of the band was becoming too grand. 'They went in a fucking macho way, and I never. They went sort of like, "We ain't gonna do this, we want five towels, we want fucking eight bars of soap, we want fucking Courvoisier," all this shit. It was bollocks to me, because I still remember my roots, where they never.' As Ozzy saw it, he was simply a working-class rock and roller from Birmingham, who happened to have hit the big time. He had never and would never believe the hype. To make matters worse, the backstage arguments were beginning to tell on them and some critics commented that the band were beginning to look tired, that they seemed to have lost the vital energy that had sent them to the top in the first place.

After the tour, the band decided to set up camp in Los Angeles again for tax reasons, but by now relations between Ozzy and Tony Iommi were at an all-time low. Iommi had long since given up the destructive drinking and drug-taking and had little time or patience with what he saw as Ozzy's self-indulgence. When the two had a furious row one day, Ozzy jumped on a plane and returned to his home in Staffordshire, where he proceeded to do little more than drink and gain weight. According to Ozzy, he was ordered back to England by Tony to try to sort himself out before they started work on another album. Drummer Bill Ward remembers it slightly differently. 'I'm not even exactly sure what happened, to be honest with you – but something happened, where Ozz took it upon himself to say, "Oh, fuck everything. I'm out of here." So he went back to his house in Staffordshire. And then we were Ozzless. That's when I think we were starting to look at other singers.'

In the summer of 1978, Ozzy briefly returned to California to rehearse for the new album *Heaven and*

Hell. The band would present him with bits and pieces, but Ozzy would claim that he had no ideas. His main response, Iommi remembers, was one of 'frustration'. Ozzy recalls those last sad days the same way. 'They asked me a couple of times before, but at the end of the day they broke down and fired me, because my heart wasn't in to what it was about. I can remember on one occasion they were all listening to these other bands and I said "This is bullshit. How come the bands that we once influenced are now influencing us?" Nobody could understand what I was talking about.'

In October 1978, they released another single, 'Hard Road'; it was to be the last single featuring Ozzy on lead vocals. It made the British Top Forty, but the record company meanwhile were knocking at the door, demanding the new album, and the three band members very quickly made up their minds that this was the end. Bill Ward was called upon to do the dirty deed, with Ronnie James Dio waiting in the wings, already lined up as Ozzy's replacement. Tony Iommi says: 'I think Ozzy had come to an end. I think he just had to sort himself out a bit. I think Ozzy was getting drunk a lot at that time. We were supposed to be rehearsing and nothing was happening and it got worse. He just started coming and going. It was like "Rehearse today? No, we'll do it tomorrow." That's how bad it got. We didn't do anything. It fizzled out. And then, when we brought Dio in, he came in with a different attitude and started singing to some of the riffs we'd got, and we thought "Oh great!" because the riffs took on life. They did work.'

The writing had been on the wall for Ozzy for some time. Maybe he couldn't see it, maybe he refused to, or maybe he knew exactly what was happening and just couldn't do a thing about it. His self-destructive streak, which had always been there since childhood, was back with a vengeance. His taste for adventure and new experiences, coupled with his inability to say no to anything or anybody, all combined to drive him close to the edge. His marriage was all but over, he had few true friends, the rest of the band were swiftly becoming strangers and the one man he would have given his life for – his father John – had died earlier that year. The death had hit Ozzy particularly hard. His father had suffered a particularly unpleasant form of bowel cancer, and for the last three months of his life was confined to a hospital bed, unable to eat. The doctors operated on him but were unable to save him and John Osbourne Senior died in his son's arms on 20 January 1978.

Ozzy recalled, many years later: 'He was stoned out of his head. I told my father one day "I take drugs." I said to him, "Before you go, will you take drugs?" He says: "I promise you I'll take drugs." He was on morphine. Totally out of his mind on morphine, because the pain must have been horrendous. I haven't got over it yet. The twentieth of January, I'll go freaking like a werewolf. I'll cry and I'll laugh all day long, because it's the day my daughter was born and the day my father died. Like a fucking lunatic.' The funeral, too, took its toll. 'It freaked me out more than anything else,' admits Ozzy. 'I was singing fucking "Paranoid" in the church, drunk, it blew me away. All my family came that I'd never seen for fucking years, and they were making comments. In England it's a weird scene at a fucking death.' Bill Ward says the band was aware of what Ozzy was going through and their hearts went out to him when his father died. When Ozzy actually left Black Sabbath, Geezer admitted he cried for two solid days. But in the end, after all the difficulties they had been through, sentiment and concern for their fragile singer was not going to be enough to hold the band together. 'I think that Ozz just got pissed off. He needed some time out. The guy was in pain,' says Bill.

'When Jack died, Ozz was extremely upset, to say the least. He was a little dysfunctional, having a tough time.'

Whatever the reasons for Ozzy's increasing reliance on drink and drugs, and the eventual disintegration of the band, there was little surprise or sympathy for him when the end finally came. He'd had more chances than most, and to many he was now little more than a washed-up drunk and druggie, a rock 'n' roll has-been whose best years were behind him. It was the end of an era. After twelve years, after selling more than twenty-five million albums and enthralling the world with some of the most original music of all time, the original Black Sabbath were no more. Ozzy had been cast adrift.

chapter four

Just Ozz

JOURNALIST: *'Do you have a drinking problem?'*
OZZY: *'Yes, I can't find a bar.'*

IT WAS TWO O'CLOCK in the afternoon. The DO NOT DISTURB sign permanently attached to the door of his hotel room meant he hadn't been bothered. Not that morning. Not any morning for several weeks, in fact. Eventually the bed's occupant groaned and rolled over. The sheets were filthy, covered in the debris of yet another night's partying: beer cans, pizza boxes and empty cigarette packets. The girl he'd picked up at the Rainbow Bar and Grill on nearby Sunset Boulevard the previous night had long since dressed and disappeared and he was on his own. Again. Briefly pausing to brush away the cigarette ash that covered the front of his shirt, he reached out and groped around under the bed amongst the growing pile of empties. Empty wine bottles, a finished whiskey bottle, used beer cans, all were pulled out and tossed back on the floor in frustration until he found the one thing was looking for – a bottle of Cognac, with just a few dregs remaining from the night before. He'd passed out before finishing it and, although most of what was left of the bottle had spilt on the floor, there was just enough there for a quick drink before he started his day's business.

Gulping it down, he yawned and stretched in anticipation of the day ahead, then sat on the end of the bed and picked up the phone. Five minutes later, his work complete, he returned to his bed. His dealer was on the way round to deliver another selection of pills and potions to see him through another day. Later on he'd maybe call down to Room Service for a fresh delivery of booze. But in the meantime, while he waited for it all to start again, he'd have another lie-down. When the drugs and drink had worn off and he came face to face with his memories, the only escape was sleep.

Since being fired from Black Sabbath, Ozzy had taken up permanent residence at the Le Parc Hotel in Los Angeles. The band didn't want him, his wife didn't want him – not surprisingly she had long since grown tired of his out-of-control ways. But Ozzy had convinced himself he didn't care. He'd picked up a five-figure check for his time in Sabbath. It wasn't much, considering the blood, sweat and tears he'd devoted to the band for the past ten years, but right now he wasn't too worried. It was enough to pay for his stay at Le Parc and, besides, he had the only friend he needed right now – a bottle of booze. 'I'd go from red wine to white wine, to whiskey to Cognac, anything – it could be horse piss as long as it got me out of my mind,' he later recalled. And he would just idle his time away, sitting gazing at the four walls, never leaving his room, never speaking to anyone.

To make matters worse, a young music fan lived directly across the road from Ozzy's hotel and every night, when he came home from work, he would throw open his windows and blast out Black Sabbath records for hours on end. It was ironic. Ozzy was drinking as hard as he could to forget, but however hard he tried there was always going to be a reminder somewhere. 'I was so fucking lonely. I thought it was the end of me,' Ozzy recalled in an interview years later. 'I couldn't possibly see me carrying on without them and I just sat around, getting severely loaded and I thought, oh well, I'll be out on the street selling hot dogs in two years' time, you know? Ozzy Osbourne? Who's he?'

Instead, into his life walked the woman who would save both his career and his life. Sharon Arden, the daughter of Black Sabbath's manager Don, was still working for her father, now in a more senior capacity than receptionist. She was managing, amongst others, Gary Moore, and Gary's drummer, Mark Nauseef, happened to be staying at Le Parc at the same time as Ozzy. The two had become friends, and when Mark was unable to make a planned rendezvous with Sharon at the hotel, he asked Ozzy to stand in for him. All he had to do, he explained, was hand over an envelope. It was important because it contained $500 (£345), so could Ozzy please make sure he kept the appointment. Ozzy agreed, but as soon as Mark walked out of the door he went straight out and bought some cocaine.

Remembering Sharon as a quiet girl who wouldn't say boo to a goose, Ozzy thought he would hear no more of it, but he had underestimated her. Sharon had grown up a lot. She had spent the past couple of years working with ELO: 'It was like running an old-age pensioners' club. They'd all been around for years and all they wanted to do on tour was sit in their rooms doing their knitting,' she complained. An older, washed-up singer no longer intimidated her, in fact she secretly relished the challenge, and the following day she came round and vented her full fury on the embarrassed star. Ozzy assumed that would be the last he would see of her, but as she left, Sharon turned round and, as a parting shot, coolly informed him that Don Arden had just fired Black Sabbath, but that they had decided they would keep him on. What's more, Sharon herself would be taking Ozzy under her wing.

Ozzy could not believe his luck, but if he thought life was going to be an easy ride with Sharon, he thought wrong. Sharon had her own personal wild streak. In the early 70s she'd drunkenly peed in the suitcase of singer Lynsey de Paul while working as a personal chaperone, simply because the two women didn't get on. She was convinced that Ozzy was a lazy drunk, squandering his talent, and that she was just the manager to do something about it. 'Ozzy had always bugged me because he was lazy, he was insecure and dumb,' she explained. 'He was like a squashed man, but I knew that he had just so much more in there, and I was just trying to kick his ass into shape. Stuck in a hotel room in Los Angeles with no band, and he just wants to sit there taking drugs. He was just not helping himself.'

With Sharon ruling him with a rod of iron, Ozzy was forced to clean up his act and start putting together a new band. He set up rehearsals at a Los Angeles studio and, with Sharon at his side, waited patiently until they had assembled the right group of musicians. After days of auditions the new band was ready. Guitarist Randy Rhoads, drummer Lee Kerslake and bass player Bob Daisley completed the line-up. Don Arden's son David, who also worked for the family business, suggested they call the band Son Of Sabbath, but Ozzy was having none of it.

It was back to basics for Ozzy. Not only was he starting out with a new band, but he also found himself in the situation he had been in when Black Sabbath first started more than ten years ago – stone broke. He'd not earned a penny for a year. The money he had been given as his pay-off was almost gone. Sharon said: 'We didn't have a credit card between us. We had no car and we were living from gig to gig.' Ozzy knew he had to earn some serious money – and fast. And the only way he knew how was by making music. Calling the band Blizzard of Ozz, he flew them to England and on 22 March 1980 they began work on Ozzy's first post-Sabbath album. The band set up camp at Ridge Farm Studios in the peaceful countryside of Surrey, and by the end of the summer the album was complete.

To test the waters, Sharon headed off to Scotland on her own and booked an unknown band called Law to play two shows at a backstreet venue in Glasgow. It was the sort of place where people would turn up on the night, hand over their money and sit and drink beer, while watching whoever happened to be booked to perform that night. For the unsuspecting punters who walked in, it was to be a night to remember. Law was actually Ozzy and the new band. Nervous about his first solo tour, he'd wanted to get a couple of concerts under his belt without the hype and hysteria that would inevitably surround his official opening night. Ozzy played the whole of the new album and a few favorite Sabbath songs. With the cheers of the crowd ringing in his ears, he left the stage in tears. He had wondered for years whether he could make it on his own. Whether the name Ozzy Osbourne alone was enough to enthrall. Now he knew for sure it was.

In September 1980 Ozzy released his first solo single, 'Crazy Train'. Still drinking heavily, and believing that few in the music industry had any interest in him anymore, Ozzy had decided not to worry about other people's expectations. Instead he would make a record that he personally loved. A record that summed him up and that he would feel proud of.

His single-mindedness paid off; his fans went wild and the song spent four weeks in the British charts. The album *Blizzard of Ozz* was released immediately; its front cover characteristically showing Ozzy in a castle, dressed in a long crimson cloak, with a skull at his side, grimacing madly while holding a large black cross above his head. His two warm-up gigs behind him, Ozzy announced his first solo tour and Britain went crazy. The *Daily Mirror* newspaper devoted a two-page spread to his return, under the headline 'The Master Of Mayhem' and fans clamored to snap up the tickets. The opening night was at the Apollo Theatre in Glasgow. Dressed in a skin-tight catsuit, Ozzy strutted on to the stage and grabbed the microphone. As the band started up at deafening level, the crowd went wild, pulling up the seats and hurling them towards the stage in a frenzy of excitement. Ozzy was back. He later recalled: 'I remember driving through Inverness in Scotland with Sharon and she turned to me and told me that the album had gone straight in at Number Fifteen in the British charts. I couldn't believe it. I thought I'd had it, you know? And I sat there and thought "Christ, I can do it on my own if I want to." I felt so much joy.'

The tour was a huge success, but Sharon was now determined to crack America, where, at the end of 1980, Ozzy was still without a record deal. At the beginning of 1981 she ordered Ozzy straight back in to the studio. While she was trying to sort things out for him in the States, it was vital that she kept her highly-strung leading man busy. She knew how Ozzy liked to spend his spare time – taking as much drink and drugs as he could – and she did not approve. In an interview a couple of years later, she explained: 'All my life I've worked in the rock and roll industry, I was born into it and obviously I've been around drug-taking all my life, because so many people in the industry take them, but it terrifies me, it's a one-way street. When I first met Ozzy he was taking a lot of drugs. They were all very, very young and it was like, "Oh, let's try it, this is fun" – it was like giving kids toys. But I hate it.'

By now Ozzy was becoming more and more dependent on Sharon. Not only had she saved his career, but she was clearly intent on saving his life, too. And, increasingly, it was becoming obvious that she had a soft spot for the long-haired lunatic that went beyond a normal manager-artist relationship. His marriage to Thelma was over in all but name, and Ozzy was finally tiring of the succession of groupies and one-night stands that had always kept him company during the long nights on the road. Eventually Ozzy decided to make his move. It will come as no surprise to discover that the evening did not feature flowers, chocolates or any traditionally romantic gesture. 'I got her drunk and leapt on her, ' the wild man of rock later admitted. 'I was never very subtle with relationships.'

Although she hated drugs, when Sharon took over Ozzy's career she, too, was enjoying her fair share of drink-induced mayhem. She was once arrested in LA for drink-driving and had to be bailed out by her close friend, Britt Ekland. She awoke the next day unaware of the incident, until Britt reminded her what had happened. Throughout those early days, her shrewd business brain kept them on the road, but for a while she found herself sucked into Ozzy's crazy world, with the pair of them quickly developing a reputation for their alcoholic outbursts. Both had strong characters and quick tempers and were not afraid to vent their feelings. Ozzy would promise not to drink so much, then promptly forget his vow and end up on another bender. Whatever commitments he had that day, be it press interviews, time in the recording studios or simply a romantic date with Sharon, would go out of the window. On one occasion Sharon was so furious that she hurled a bottle of perfume straight at Ozzy's head. Too drunk to get out of the way in time, it hit him full on and a doctor had to be called out to treat him for concussion. 'Our fights were legendary,' she recalled later. 'We'd beat the shit out of each other. At a gig, Ozzy would run off stage during a guitar solo to fight with me, then run back on to finish the song. We were in the gutter, morally, and I realized that if we both carried on, we'd wind up a washed-up pair of old drunks, living in a hovel somewhere.' Maybe figuring that Ozzy was doing enough drinking for the both of them, she promptly quit and began to concentrate on what she did best – managing her errant partner.

Musically, she respected Ozzy hugely, but away from work she found him kind, funny and charismatic, with a surprisingly gentle side. 'He's a legend,' she once explained. 'I admire him and I love him.' In her devotion she would patiently tolerate the worst of his alcohol-induced behavior. On one occasion she flew to Tokyo to meet up with him on tour. After the show she was overcome with jetlag and went straight back to the hotel. Ozzy at the time was trying to stay off drink, so Sharon didn't worry too much when he said he would stay on for the post-gig party. Five hours later she was woken by the sound of giggling at the hotel room door. She opened it to find a drunken Ozzy struggling to fit the key in the lock, accompanied by a pretty Japanese girl. Ozzy, it emerged, had ended up in a nightclub where he had downed the best part of a bottle of sake. Forgetting that Sharon was there, he had invited the girl back to his room. Furious, Sharon punched the girl and then pulled a painting down from the wall and smashed it over Ozzy's head. 'It's funny now,' Sharon recalled in an interview many years after the event. 'It wasn't then.'

As Ozzy worked away back at Ridge Farm Studios, putting together a second album, Sharon was busy plotting in America. By March 1981 Jet Records had agreed to release Ozzy's first album in the States, but it was to be with the minimum of fuss and publicity and, what's more, they would only pay him $65,000 (£44,800). Ozzy and Sharon reluctantly agreed. The album, of course, went on to become a huge hit – having already hit the Top Ten in the British charts, it reached Number Twenty-One in America, going Quadruple Platinum in just a few months. Ozzy and Sharon felt vindicated, but both agreed that what Ozzy needed right now was a headline tour and some major publicity to raise his profile even higher. Sharon did her bit. With her tough manager's head on, she insisted that Ozzy would not appear as a support act for other bands, instead he would concentrate on heading the bill at smaller 3,000-seater stadiums. Then she set about re-vamping Ozzy's look. His trademark white cat-suit, designed by his first wife Thelma, was consigned to the bin. Ozzy's whole image, declared Sharon, was out of date and way too 1970s. Overnight his hair was dyed blonde, he began to wear much heavier make-up, and elaborate, brightly-colored outfits became the norm.

The rest was down to Ozzy. Jet Records and its distributor, CBS Columbia, had invited the singer along to one of their regular conventions. These were informal gatherings where record company executives could actually meet and chat with the bands on their label. In truth, CBS were not desperately interested in Ozzy at that time; they'd just signed up Adam Ant who had become a huge star in Britain, and they were keen to put all their energies into promoting him. But the meeting with Ozzy and Sharon wasn't going to take long, they reckoned, a handshake, a quick drink and a little small talk was all that was required – or so they thought.

The problem was that Ozzy wasn't very good at small talk. To quash his nerves before the meeting he had already drunk half a bottle of whiskey. The drink, combined with a publicity stunt that Sharon had secretly cooked up, was to prove a deadly combination. Sharon was desperate for the record company executives to sit up and take notice of Ozzy. In her eyes they were ignoring and under-promoting a huge and unique talent. To grab their attention she decided that Ozzy should walk into the room and take two doves out of his pocket. He would fool around with them for a while; maybe pretend to bite the head off one, before throwing the birds in the air. It would surprise the record company executives and cause a bit of a stir and, naturally, there was to be a photographer on hand who would be able to capture the moment and release the pictures to newspapers and magazines. It would guarantee Ozzy some much-needed American press attention, Sharon reckoned.

Sharon handed the doves to Ozzy just before the meeting and he hid them in his coat pocket, as arranged. When he entered the room he sat on the arm of the chair and, as instructed by Sharon, took the doves out. Sharon recalls: 'He let two of them fly off and all these silly girls were sitting there smiling and sighing quietly, and then Ozzy grabs the last dove and yanks its head off, I couldn't believe my eyes.' With blood dripping out of his mouth and on to his trousers, Ozzy dropped the dove's bloody, still-flapping body on to the meeting table in front of him. As horrified executives threw up, Ozzy was escorted from the building and told never to come back. 'It was fucking great' he joked, years later. 'It tasted like a good hamburger.'

How much of the incident was the impulsive act of a crazed madman and how much was a calculated publicity stunt, we will never know. Most likely it was a potent combination of the two. There was little Ozzy wouldn't do to shock, he still got that boyish thrill from offending figures of authority and, at the same time, the incident would set him apart forever from the whole swathe of other rock singers desperately fighting to get noticed.

An eyewitness from Epic is convinced that the whole horrific event was definitely pre-planned and that Sharon, too, was in on the stunt. 'It was not a spontaneous act. He didn't just walk in and happen to find a dove hanging out in the CBS reception area and say, "Gee, I'll take this in with me in case I get hungry and they don't have coffee or donuts." It was right in his jacket pocket. I'm ninety-nine and nine-tenths sure it was alive. I remember I was leaning forward and thinking, "How cute" and suddenly he bites its head off. There was blood on the floor. I think he ate the head; he started spitting some feathers out. I was in shock. It's hard to remember too much after that, to tell you the truth. It was horrible.'

But while the CBS executives were less than impressed by the stunt, the whole of America descended into an Ozzy frenzy. The story had naturally leaked out, photos and all, and newspaper and magazines all over the country were soon full of stories of the outrageous Oz. TV and radio clamored to interview him or anyone who had witnessed the event. Suddenly everyone had an opinion about the controversial singer. The Humane Society of America started a determined campaign to ban him from any live performance in the States, while his teenage fans revelled in the new-found notoriety of their hero.

Love him or hate him, Ozzy was no longer just another heavy rock singer, he was an extraordinary personality, a crazy eccentric, a legend. Sharon and Ozzy just couldn't believe their luck. 'It was all so perfect really,' recalls Sharon. 'We had stayed up till four o'clock in the morning the night before the convention, trying to dream up an idea for something Ozzy could do that would make everyone remember him. And, finally, when we came up with doves, I still thought he was half-joking about biting its head off. But believe me, it really worked for us.'

chapter five

Bat Out of Hell?

6 *To be honest, I am a little bit crazy. I accept that. I've always been outrageous. I've never been the everyday you. I've always gone over the top with everything.* 9

THE DOVE EPISODE had given Ozzy a taste for publicity. It also seemed to have given him a taste for small inedible creatures and in 1982 came the incident that was to haunt him for the rest of his life. It followed on from ten months of controversy in which the legend of Ozzy the wild man grew with every public appearance.

In 1981, biting the head off a dove had brought Ozzy to the attention of the few remaining people in Britain and America who still hadn't heard of him and his first US solo tour was going down an absolute storm. Two weeks into the tour his showcase concert at the New York Palladium was announced and the box office opened with 3,000 tickets. By the end of that afternoon every single ticket had gone. Many wanted to see just how Ozzy was coping without the boys from Black Sabbath. For others, it was the first chance to see a live rendition of Ozzy's new material from his first solo album *Blizzard of Ozz*. But for many, it was the opportunity to see a live show, the like of which they would probably never again witness in their lives.

Dry ice and gothic imagery was only half of it. Ozzy had also decided to send mail shots out to the towns where he would be appearing later on in the tour. The leaflets encouraged concertgoers to bring along raw meat to throw at the singer during the show. 'It read something like "Bring your liver to an Ozzy show – and he'll throw it back at you,"' Ozzy recalls. His days working in the Birmingham abattoir had shown that Ozzy wasn't in the slightest bit squeamish. Far from it – in fact he seemed to have a macabre and childlike fascination with blood and guts that his audiences, mainly comprising male heavy metal fans under the age of twenty-five, seemed to share. 'The way I put it out is audience participation, it's like a horror show, so people bring along whatever they want to bring along,' Ozzy explained later. 'You can do anything at the show as long as you don't harm yourself. Have some fun. I don't mind a bit of liver or a bit of steak thrown at me on stage – do it, it's great fun.'

At the same time Ozzy had it written into his contract that each venue would provide $36 (£25) worth of calves' livers and pigs' intestines. A huge catapult was then installed on the stage with a bucket full of the rotting offal loaded on to it. Halfway through the show, Ozzy would give the signal and the contents were fired out into the screaming audience. It was the cue for them to retaliate and the contents of every butcher's shop for miles around would come flying back on to the stage. But eager to outdo their hero, the heavy metal audiences would not stop there. As well as raw meat, dead animals were now being thrown on to the stage every night, including rats, snakes, lizards and even cats. One night a huge swamp frog landed on its back right in front of him. The creature was so big that, for a terrible moment, Ozzy thought a baby had been tossed on to the stage. At another concert a fan was refused entry after turning up carrying an ox's head under his arm.

After one show the promoters received a phone call from a concerned mother asking how to get the blood out of clothes, but generally the audience loved it. During the encore the group were now ritually pelted with cow's eyes, livers and lungs and the more offal that landed on the stage, the better Ozzy judged his performance to have been. With by now the biggest following of his career, Ozzy was on a high. He was still taking drugs and drinking, but far less so than in previous years; for now the thrill of live performance was giving him all the buzz he needed. The new band had given him reason to carry on and had helped him realize his dreams. Or as Ozzy himself put it: 'Right now my only ambition left in life is to go to Egypt, stand on top of the Central Pyramid and piss all over it!'

By the late summer of 1981 *Blizzard of Ozz* had notched up its first million sales and Ozzy picked up his first solo platinum album. As more and more dates were added to the tour at bigger and bigger venues, Sharon decided it was time to capitalize on the never-ending demand for the singer by releasing his second album *Diary of A Madman*. The timing was perfect. It quickly stormed to Number Fourteen in the British album charts and Number Sixteen in the States, creating a whole new raft of headlines for the delighted couple. The album cover showed Ozzy wild-haired and wild-eyed, in ripped and apparently blood-stained jeans, his arms outstretched towards the viewer. Cobwebs festooned a chandelier and on the far wall hung an upside-down cross. In the far corner, by a gothic arched window, sat a small giggling boy, actually his son Louis, on the table beside him a clearly dead bird.

By now Ozzy had fallen head-over-heels for Sharon, but amidst the euphoria of the tour and being in love, he was going through a painful divorce from his first wife Thelma, back home in Britain. Things had been bad between them for years and Ozzy had a habit of disappearing to friends' houses for days or even weeks on end without telling Thelma where he was. The end came when he staggered home drunk one day to find all his belongings outside the house. Thelma shouted from an upstairs window that if he attempted to enter the house she would call the police and he would be arrested. She had given him more last chances than he deserved, she was filing for divorce and wanted nothing more to do with him. Ozzy was devastated; although he had behaved badly on tour, he had never meant to hurt Thelma, and he tortured himself with thoughts of how different things could have been. He blamed himself for the break-up and, rather than go through the agony of a protracted divorce, he agreed to hand everything over to her without so much as a murmur of complaint.

Even so, the proceedings took their toll. Already wrecked by the American tour, he arrived in London in November 1981 to begin a British tour, but found to his dismay that he could not cope with it – either physically or mentally. 'I got into a divorce, which wasn't very funny. No matter what anybody says, a divorce just knocks the wind out of your sails and I couldn't cope with the pressure of the work and dealing with that,' he says. 'I was going through this big emotional trauma, all to do with the fact that for the first time in my life, I had actually fallen in love. And then, while I'm still trying to sort that one out, we're starting the British tour, my first wife's divorcing me, and I just started drinking more and more.' Ozzy performed two gigs in characteristic style. In Bristol he appeared for an encore wearing nothing but his underwear, and the following night in Cardiff fans pelted him with dead crows. But these shows were all he could manage and, to the dismay of his British fans, the rest of the tour was cancelled. Ozzy returned to America to take a month off and lick his wounds, but two months later, in January 1982, he was back on tour again in the States.

Black Sabbath had never exactly been subtle, but when Oz came to town, things moved on to a different plane entirely. The stage setting for the Diary of a Madman tour was a huge castle, complete with fog. The drummer performed on a raised platform and there was an opening in the center of the stage where a dwarf would come out to hand Ozzy drinks and towels. Nicknamed Ronnie (his real name was John Allen), the dwarf, dressed in a macabre, medieval outfit, would have pigs' entrails hurled at him every time he appeared and would be stuffed kicking and screaming back into the hole. The show's finale would see Ozzy, dressed in a red chain mail cat suit, act out a grand execution of the dwarf in which he was 'hanged' by the neck from a noose. The 'execution' actually involved a harness and no harm ever came to Ronnie, but that didn't stop the establishment howling their disapproval. Neither did the spectacle impress the new wave of more fashionable bands making their assault on both the British and American charts. But Ozzy, typically, couldn't have cared less. 'I'm sick and tired of these pseuds with their spiky hairy cuts and they're getting nowhere,' he said vehemently. 'I'm still as crazy as ever. I still go on the stage and do my best to be a bit more crazy every day. I guarantee if people come and see this show they'll be talking about it for years. I live out a lot of people's fantasies. It's so amazing.'

Had Ozzy's critics any inkling of what was coming next, they really wouldn't have worried about the faked hanging of a dwarf. Ironically, the incident that was to create the biggest furore in Ozzy's entire career was not something that he had actually planned. During this tour, as in previous tours, audiences continued to hurl liberal quantities of rotting offal and dead animals at Ozzy during his performance and fans were now adding rubber snakes and plastic rats to their offerings. So on 20 January when a bat was flung at his feet during a show at Des Moines, Iowa, Ozzy didn't give it a second thought. The bat lay motionless – it was actually stunned by the bright lights – but Ozzy, assuming it was plastic, decided to play to the crowd, picked it up, put its head in his mouth and took a huge bite. When the terrified creature started to wriggle, a horrified Ozzy realized what he had done. 'Sharon told me later that she saw its wings flapping from the side of the stage, but I didn't,'

Ozzy was to recount later. 'I just picked it up and put it in my mouth in the excitement of the show. I mean, fuck me, biting a bat's bloody off! It's not very nice to taste – a fresh bat's head – it's all crunchy and warm.'

The crowd went wild and journalists at the concert rushed for the phones to report the incredible incident they had just witnessed. But Ozzy had other things on his mind. He had no idea where the creature had originally come from – whether it was a pet, from the zoo or from the wild – and in his mind a bat could mean only one thing – rabies. As soon as the show was over, Ozzy was rushed to hospital for a series of injections. Deep down he was terrified, but he coped with his fear in the only way he knew how – with typical Ozzy humor – barking like a dog as he lay on the hospital trolley waiting for the first needle. And when a worried Sharon appeared at his bedside amidst the doctors and nurses and asked how he was, Ozzy couldn't help but quip: 'If I've got rabies, you'll soon know. I'll start sniffing dogs' asses.' But rabies injections are not a laughing matter, and the shots – in his buttocks, arms, legs and stomach – went on for a week. To make matters worse, Ozzy reacted badly to the vaccine, which caused him to faint and collapse several times during the following week's shows. Fans anxious to know exactly what it felt like to bite the head off a bat, were told by Ozzy that it was one of the most painful experiences of his life. 'If you want to be a complete dick, try it,' he told them, adding that the anti-rabies treatment was 'like having a golf ball injected into your ass.'

In truth, it turned out to be nothing compared with what he was about to go through. America and Britain went into meltdown. While fans rushed out to get bat tattoos, the good citizens of America rose up against the singer, accusing him of every crime under the sun. In every city, when Ozzy arrived for a concert there would be pickets and demonstrations as well as predictable fury in the local media. A letter published in the local paper in Omaha summed up the nation's mood. 'This weekend's concert by Ozzy Osbourne should be banned for the sake of the community's mental health,' the writer urged. 'This music and what it represents is truly evil. Nothing good can come of it. The writing is on the wall. The negative aspects of this type of music are already apparent.' Officials immediately introduced security checks at every venue to search concertgoers for live animals, and representatives from the Humane Society began to monitor the shows. Dart Anthony, head of the Humane Society of Southern Nevada, who turned up at Ozzy's Las Vegas concert, told waiting reporters: 'This guy's gimmick is young animals and blood. It is not the kind of image we need for this town.'

Meanwhile, rumors of Ozzy's excesses began to spread wildly. As if the bat incident weren't enough, there were suggestions that he had tossed a litter of puppies into the audience at a concert in San Francisco and refused to continue playing until the audience had killed them and thrown them back. Nobody at the concert ever came forward to say they had witnessed anything of the sort, and Ozzy's publicist at the time insisted: 'These rumors are nothing but rumors. The kids started them. They're avid, sick individuals. It's just a rock and roll show. He made a mistake and we wish they'd leave him alone.' Meanwhile, a goat society in Michigan ordered its members not to sell a goat to anyone with a British accent, following a rumor that Ozzy was planning to blow one up on stage. The fact that none of it was true didn't really matter. It all added to the image of Ozzy as a psychotic madman and, while thousands queued up to demonstrate against him, Sharon was adding more and more dates to the end of the tour as thousands more lined up for tickets to see the living legend in action.

To help counteract some of the bad publicity, Ozzy donated $36,000 (£25,000) of his own money to the American Society for the Prevention of Cruelty to Animals, but this gesture was not enough to assuage the anger of Middle America. As the tour continued through the Southern states he arrived at one venue to find 500 angry locals picketing the show, with placards denouncing the singer as a Satanist. Most other singers would have heeded the warning and turned round and got the hell out of town. But not Ozzy. Instead he climbed down from the tour bus, got a board of his own, nailed it to a sweeping brush and joined the demonstration. 'I joined in the procession and started singing "We Shall Overcome" and they didn't even know it was me at the end of the queue!' Ozzy later recalled with a chuckle.

His plans to bring the tour to Britain were, not surprisingly, scuppered when Ozzy revealed that far from toning the show down, he actually planned to liven it up a bit, with flamethrowers, the road crew dressed as Quasimodo with humps and tights, and a finale which appeared to show Ozzy being blown to pieces. At the same time, the Royal Society for the Prevention of Cruelty to Animals warned that forthwith they would monitor all his British shows to make sure no birds or animals were ill treated. Ozzy's response was typically unrepentant. 'With all this hounding, somebody should start a society to prevent cruelty to me!' he quipped. At a concert in Germany a few years later, he was similarly unembarrassed about his behavior, and when a pious official warned him that in his country they would not tolerate Ozzy biting the head off a bat on stage he came back, quick as a flash: 'You've got to be fucking joking. You killed half the world.'

By now, in many American states Ozzy was a virtual outlaw and on one occasion his tour bus was pulled over by the police who quizzed the driver as to whether

Ozzy was aboard. Although the singer was fast asleep in the back the quick-thinking driver told them that Ozzy never traveled by bus and always flew. The officers believed the driver, but decided to arrest him anyway, simply because he was part of the Ozzy entourage. He was given a police escort to the station and taken in for questioning, so Ozzy woke that morning to find himself parked up outside the local police station. The driver was eventually released and returned to the bus and drove off, much to Ozzy's glee. But while he might have got one over on the police on this occasion, his next brush with the law was to end in much more serious trouble.

The British weekly rock paper *Melody Maker* had sent a reporter and photographer to America to catch up with Ozzy on tour. The band had just arrived in San Antonio, Texas and the photographer thought it would be a good idea to take Ozzy out to the Alamo to pose for pictures. Ozzy's drinking was once again as heavy as ever. Sharon had tried everything she could think of to persuade him to give up, or at least cut down, but nothing had worked. She watched him like a hawk when she was around, but needed to devise a way of preventing him from drinking when she wasn't. She'd already instructed the tour hotels that on no account should any booze be delivered on room service to their suites. In a moment of inspiration she came up with the bright idea of taking away Ozzy's clothes. She figured that even Ozzy wouldn't dare go out naked to bars, so, without anything to wear, he'd have to stay in his room and drink coffee. What Sharon hadn't counted on was Ozzy's determination to get a drink at all costs, and his amazing ingenuity. If his own clothes weren't around, he reasoned, he would simply put on hers.

'I was alone in my hotel room in San Antonio and I wanted the hair of the dog, so I put one of her dresses on. I'm walking around the town with this green evening dress on, slurping from a bottle of Courvoisier, drunk as an idiot,' Ozzy recalls. Recalling his pre-arranged meeting with the photographer at the Alamo, Ozzy weaved his way over there. The photographer couldn't believe the sight in front of him, Ozzy swaying around with a bottle in his hand, dressed up as a woman, but Ozzy persuaded him that it would just make the pictures even funnier and that they should go ahead. 'And that was my big downfall,' Ozzy recalls. 'I was as drunk as a skunk, and when you're drunk like that you tend to piss a lot. The pictures were taking a while, so I stopped to take a leak. I spotted this bit of old tumbled-down brick wall and I thought that would do . . .'

It did; but the tumbled-down wall was actually part of the Alamo building – a sacred national shrine and a living testament to the brave Texans who sacrificed their lives in the fight for Texan independence from Mexico. In mid-stream, Ozzy found himself the object of a torrent of abuse from a furious official. 'He's screaming – "You dirty bastard, you filthy motherfucker, you son of a bitch, you filthy faggot. Ain't cha got no respect?"' Ozzy recalls. 'The old guy is ranting and raving away about national shrines and pissing and he's screaming and waving his hands in the air and I'm standing there in my dress trying to calm the poor bugger down.' While Ozzy was being read the riot act by the outraged official, his colleague called the police and within minutes two armed officers had arrived on the scene. After the lengthy history lesson from the old man, Ozzy fully realized the enormity of what he had done and, when the police began to question him, he decided that honesty was the best policy. He admitted that yes, he had been caught short and he had been forced to relieve himself on the Alamo. 'But it was a genuine mistake and, anyway, when the Mexicans were attacking it there must have been more than just piss running down the walls!' he couldn't help adding. Ozzy's response proved a bit too honest for the police, who promptly arrested him, bundled him in to the back of a police van and drove him to the station where he was unceremoniously thrown in a cell. As the arresting officer told him as the cell door swung firmly shut behind him: 'Son, when you piss on the Alamo, you piss on the state of Texas.'

As if he weren't in enough trouble already, Ozzy looked round to discover that he was sharing his cell with a huge and very angry Texan, who had been arrested for murdering his wife. Ozzy, still in his dress, with make-up running down his face and his long hair looking more unkempt than ever, thought his days were numbered. The man sat and simply stared menacingly at Ozzy for several minutes, but eventually broke the silence by asking him gruffly who he was and what he'd been arrested for. When Ozzy sheepishly explained what had happened the man became hysterical. Convinced he was about to be beaten up by a patriotic Texan, outraged by a Brit in a dress who had violated a State shrine, Ozzy cowered in the corner. His cellmate rushed forward towards Ozzy and he winced in anticipation. When he opened his eyes, it was to the bizarre spectacle of this huge bear of a man holding his hand and repeatedly pumping it up and down. It turned out the Texan was a huge Ozzy Osbourne fan and just hadn't recognized his hero in a dress. Overcome by excitement, he was convinced that Ozzy was his savior and insisted on spending the next two hours telling Ozzy the full details of his crime. On his release, he insisted, Ozzy must go straight to the State Governor and help clear his name. When Ozzy was eventually released, however, he had enough on his plate clearing his own name. He appeared before a judge in a local court of law, where he was fined and banned from ever playing in San Antonio, Texas, again – a ban that was only lifted in 1992.

Undeterred, Ozzy continued with the tour. He may have made a whole new raft of enemies in Texas, but the news of his latest misdemeanor was music to his fans' ears. The dead animal count at the end of every show was increasing and at one venue some Satanist fans even slaughtered a cat outside the hall before the show began. Right-wing Christian groups were now mingling with supporters of the Humane Society outside the venues, handing out leaflets denouncing the singer and, in Boston, the Humane Society actually managed to get the concert banned. It was only when Sharon went back to court and appealed that the decision was overturned. When the Boston show finally went ahead, there was complete pandemonium. Hundreds of journalists and TV crews jostled for space alongside sinister-looking black-clad heavy metal fans and security guards. 'You'd have thought someone had assassinated the President,' Ozzy recalls. Before he went on stage, he was handed a piece of paper with a list of bans which, if ignored, would mean instant arrest. If he made any suggestive sexual movements he would be hauled off; if he made any statements concerning the injury or death of any animals he would be off; and if he used foul language he could expect the same fate. Reading the list in the presence of armed guards, Ozzy cheekily asked: 'Is it okay if I sing?' The furious police officer who had handed him the sheet was not amused and threatened him with a beating, but Ozzy just roared with laughter. After all the scrapes he had been in, it would take far more than a humorless cop to upset his day. Grinning from ear to ear, he made for the stage and the appreciative screams of the ecstatic crowd. The American police might not understand him, but his teenage fans certainly did.

In St Louis the mayhem was even worse. Following his arrest in San Antonio, Ozzy was quoted as saying that his next ambition was to relieve himself on the steps of the White House. He later claimed he couldn't remember whether he'd actually made the remark or not – quite possible, considering Ozzy's daily intake of alcohol in those days. The St Louis authorities, however, chose to believe that he had made this threat. Not knowing what to expect next from this crazy guy, more than a hundred armed and uniformed police officers ringed the concert stage, ready to act at the first sign of anti-social behavior. Officials from the Humane Society supervised the show to ensure there was no cruelty to animals, while armed officers from the FBI infiltrated the audience and backstage areas.

Offstage, Ozzy tried to live as normal a life as possible, but his notoriety meant he now had to be accompanied everywhere by a burly bodyguard – a former Vietnam veteran who clearly wouldn't stand any nonsense from anyone. Just how essential the bodyguard was to his safety, Ozzy discovered very quickly. Bored, but trying to cut down on his alcohol intake, he had decided to take a gentle stroll to a coffee shop one afternoon, to while away a couple of hours before the evening show. The place was busy, so Ozzy and his guard ordered their drinks then squeezed themselves in to a quiet corner table. Minding their own business, they chatted for a while, before taking out their newspapers and starting to read. After several minutes, the place fell silent. Ozzy looked up and realized to his horror that he had been spotted. 'Someone in a suit and tie started screaming, "Put Jesus in front of you". All the other people in the restaurant turned out to be in a party with him and so they all joined in,' Ozzy remembers. 'Then this Rambo guy who's with me goes into kill mode and starts throwing them all through the window. I had to crawl out of there, literally on my hands and knees.' On another occasion, after driving for eight hours across the deserted Midwest, Ozzy's tour bus pulled up at a truck stop in the early hours of the morning. The place was empty, so Ozzy was amazed when a man approached him and handed him a leaflet headed 'Jesus Saves'. 'And I say to the guy "Where did you come from? There's nothing for miles and miles around here."' When the earnest young man explained that he'd been following behind the bus in his car all night, Ozzy's response was unequivocal. 'You've been following the bus all night just to give me this fucking piece of paper? You don't want to go to a church, my friend. You want to go see a fucking psychiatrist!'

To whip up even more interest in Ozzy, Sharon had begun to organize album signings at the major stores in the various cities along the tour. In San Francisco 3,000 fans, mostly fourteen- to sixteen-year-olds, queued outside a record store to meet their idol and receive an autograph. After five hours, with Ozzy still nowhere near reaching the end of the line, hundreds of the teenagers broke away from the queue, climbed up on to the roof of the record shop and smashed their way in. In Toronto, amidst similar scenes, 4,000 fans ran wild and smashed their way through shop windows in an attempt to get to the front. When Ozzy reached Los Angeles, the authorities, fearful of further disturbances, banned him from all public appearances. He was too wild, they declared, too unpredictable, and far too bad an influence on the young people of their city.

Ozzy had always been an eccentric. As a young man he would act first and ask questions later. His sense of humor was undoubtedly juvenile and, at times, veered on the tasteless and crude, but it was never malicious. And while the establishment didn't really appreciate the difference, there was a growing number of people who did. Now, to Ozzy's utter amazement and joy, his crazy behavior was positively beginning to pay off. The more outrageous he was, the more his fans adored him and the higher his public profile rose. And even if *he* wanted to quieten down, his audiences just wouldn't allow it. They paid good money to see the wild man of rock and they expected him to stop at nothing to shock. In an interview a year later, in 1983, Ozzy admitted: 'If I'm not up to some crazy prank, if I'm not hanging off a ship's mast or something, they think there's something wrong with me. If I sat down and just looked out of the window they'd say, "Are you okay, Ozzy? You're not ill? You're not setting fire to the chicken pen today, you're not killing the cats, you're not blowing the car up or shooting a horse in the shed."'

For some singers, keeping up such an image could have been an exhausting business. But for Ozzy it was simple, the stage persona being just an extension of his real-life character. 'I'm not crazy, but I like doing off-the-wall things,' he once explained. 'There are so many out there that get up in the morning, say "Good morning, darling", have a piece of toast, shave, bathroom, coat on, "See you tonight", come home from work, take your coat off, quick pint round the pub, read the paper, go home, watch the news, slippers on, bed. That ain't for me.'

chapter six

Till Death Us Do Part

❝ People say my legacy is that everyone would like
to be Ozzy for a day. But if they were Ozzy for a day
they'd soon change their minds. ❞

JUST THREE MONTHS into 1982 and Ozzy was on a high. Sure, he was in trouble with the American authorities in just about every State, but his two solo albums were flying high, his fans were snapping up concert tickets quicker than they could be printed and he was doing what he loved best – playing music and playing the fool. He also had Sharon – as a manager he trusted her implicitly, and as a girlfriend he loved her as he'd never loved anyone in his life before. The icing on the cake was that he was touring with a bunch of guys he adored, including the immensely talented Randy Rhoads. Ozzy and Randy had become extremely close in the three years since they met; they respected each other musically and shared the same sense of humor. Ozzy couldn't believe that things could get any better. Or that anything could now possibly go wrong. Sadly, he was to be proved wrong on both counts and, by the end of the year, Ozzy was to have experienced the most unbearable tragedy and the most incredible happiness in the space of just a few short months.

Ozzy and Randy had gelled from the first second they met. Skinny – Randy was the proud owner of a twenty-two-inch waist – and good-looking, with long blond hair and a sunny temperament, Randy looked every inch the 1980s rock star. But he was gentle and modest, without the typical rock star ego. And, what mattered most to Ozzy was the young musician's amazing talent. He had the meanest hook on a Gibson Electric guitar that Ozzy had ever heard. What's more he was bright and ambitious. At the age of just seventeen he'd formed his own

105

band, Quiet Riot, supplementing his income by teaching guitar at a Los Angeles college. Eight years younger than Ozzy, he was the perfect foil and the pair formed a lethal partnership – Ozzy the vaudeville frontman, Randy his loud lead guitarist, whose touch turned every song to gold. Other band members came and went during those tours of the early 80s, but Ozzy and Randy stuck together like glue. For Ozzy it was like the early days of Black Sabbath, only better. He had found a kindred spirit, someone who instinctively shared his dreams. As Sharon recalls: 'It was an unbelievable time to be working with Ozzy and Randy. The whole thing that was beginning to grow between the two of them on stage was really astounding.'

But on 19 March 1982 all that was to change for ever. Ozzy and the band had played a show the previous night in Knoxville, Tennessee and were now firmly ensconced on their tour bus en route to Orlando, Florida, where they were to appear in a concert alongside Foreigner and UFO. Randy and Ozzy sat chatting happily at the back of the bus in the early hours of the morning. They talked excitedly about the band's success so far and discussed the upcoming concerts. By now they were relaxed enough with each other to share their hopes and dreams. Ozzy confided in Randy that he wanted to be the biggest rock star on the planet, while Randy told Ozzy that one day he planned to leave rock music to pursue a degree in classical music at UCLA. Eventually, when neither could keep his eyes open any longer, they crawled off to their respective bunks. It was around three in the morning and everyone was fast asleep except the bus's driver, Andrew Aycock. His ex-wife had turned up at Ozzy's gig the previous night and had ended up traveling on the bus back to Florida. Sharon wasn't very keen to give her a lift, as the bus was already packed tight with people sleeping in every available space, but she had reluctantly agreed.

Aycock and his ex-wife weren't on good terms. They had gone through a messy divorce and, as Andrew drove through the night, she sat at his shoulder, the two of them arguing and bickering. Aycock had been taking cocaine to help him stay awake and, when he finally stopped the bus at 8 am, he had had no sleep and an exhausting night dissecting his failed marriage.

Aycock had pulled up at the bus depot at Leesburg, Florida. The depot was little more than a bare patch of land with three buildings arranged around a large field. There was a landing strip for helicopters and small light aircraft, some of which were housed in the buildings. While Aycock waited for repairs to be carried out on the bus, he told the few passengers who were now awake that he had once been a professional pilot and that he was happy to take a few of them up for a spin in a Beechcraft Bonanza airplane. What he didn't add was that his licence had actually been revoked after he was held responsible for the death of a small boy in a helicopter accident years earlier. Unaware of this, tour manager Jake Duncan and keyboard player Don Airey jumped at the chance of some mid-air acrobatics to liven up the morning as they waited for the bus to be fixed. Aycock showed off doing some loops and eventually brought the plane back down.

The ex-pilot then extended the invitation to the only other two people awake on the bus, Randy Rhoads and the tour's fifty-four-year-old seamstress Rachael Youngblood. Both were terrified of flying. Earlier on in the tour, the band had enjoyed a five-day break in their schedule and everyone but Randy had flown to Los Angeles for some rest. Randy had chosen to stay put because he didn't want to set foot on a plane if he could possibly avoid it. But Aycock told Randy and Rachael what fun it would be to take a spin and eventually they were persuaded to have a go.

What happened next is not entirely clear; there are

conflicting eyewitness accounts and most of the band and tour entourage were asleep during those fateful moments, but what is known is that, after circling the bus three times, the plane dived a fourth time, clipping the bus and crashing into a nearby house, where it exploded in flames. There were reports that Randy and Rachael had been fooling around in the plane shortly before it crashed, but Sharon is certain that their mutual fear of flying meant this would never have happened. 'What Ozzy and I are convinced happened is this: this stupid ex-pilot cowboy took them up in the plane and his ex-wife was stood by the bus. She'd got off the bus and she was standing there watching the plane fly around. And we think that for one split second the pilot said "Fuck you" and went for it.' Ozzy and Sharon jumped out of their beds at the sound of the crash and rushed outside. Ozzy could not believe his eyes, and when one of the shocked garage staff told him that a deaf man lived in the house hit by the plane, he rushed in, fought his way through the flames and pulled the stunned old man to safety.

All three in the plane were killed instantly. Randy was only twenty-four and Ozzy was devastated. In one split second he'd lost the best friend he'd ever had in his life – the man who had become like a younger brother to him. 'I was very, very sad. Not only did Randy die but our seamstress Rachael died with him, she had been with us since the word go,' Ozzy explained much later. 'The day that happened was a day I'll never forget. It was the most horrific thing in the world that ever happened to me, because he was a sweet man and she was a sweet woman.'

At Randy's funeral, a stunned Ozzy, making a rare appearance in a suit and tie, helped carry the young man's coffin. Not since his father died had he felt so grief-stricken, so unable to carry on. For all his charisma and bravado Ozzy was a deeply sensitive man. He had few close buddies, but those he did count as his real friends meant the world to him. Without Randy around, his own life seemed pointless and bleak. Ozzy told Sharon that he could not go on with the band or the tour. His career as a rock star was over. To make matters worse, he couldn't help but torment himself with the thought that he, too, could so easily have perished on the doomed joy flight. If he hadn't been so late to bed the previous night, if he hadn't been sleeping off yet another hangover, he would have been larking around with Randy and the guys as well. 'This has gone through my head a thousand and one times,' Ozzy admitted in an interview several years later. 'Had I been awake, I would have been on that plane, probably sitting on the fucking wing.'

Sharon knew she had to do something. And fast. While Ozzy might feel he could no longer face making music, Sharon knew that music would be the only thing that would save him. Three weeks later she forced a reluctant Ozzy to hold auditions for a new guitarist. They signed up the first decent player that came along and, within three weeks, were back on the road again. But it was a difficult time. Audiences were turning up carrying huge banners bearing touching tributes to Randy. Ozzy was just about holding it together on stage, but during the day was going to pieces. What's more, the fans' antics that had amused Ozzy so much just a few months earlier were now beginning to get him down. Audiences had taken to throwing bottles and fireworks around the hall during shows. It was all getting out of control. One night Sharon was rushed to hospital after a firework exploded at her feet. The explosion left her temporarily blind and deaf and she had to be treated for serious cuts to her neck. Meanwhile, Ozzy's detractors were still out in force. He was in huge demand with local television stations along the route, but he would often find himself ambushed, with interviewers suddenly producing religious leaders in the studio to confront him without warning. He started to receive death threats, and at the concerts stranger and stranger people were beginning to join the audience, including Devil-worshipers demanding his autograph in blood. Security was tripled at every venue and the singer was told it would be unwise to go out without bodyguards.

Depressed, Ozzy predictably took refuge in drink and drugs, but Sharon, who had never approved of Ozzy's gargantuan drugs intake, was determined to put a stop to Ozzy's self-destructive habits. 'The only way I could hope to control Ozzy was to literally end up having these horrendous fist fights with him all over America,' she recalls. 'I'd discover where he'd hidden his awful bag of coke or whatever, and so I'd throw it down the toilet or out of the window. Then he'd find out and he'd beat me up and I'd beat him up and it just went on and on like that for months.' On one occasion, in San Diego, Ozzy splashed out on a huge bag of cocaine. After snorting half the bag he went for a walk to get some fresh air, but when he returned Sharon was waiting for him. She knew exactly what he'd been up to and, before he knew it, a potted plant had come flying through the air and hit him on the head. She then grabbed what remained of the bag of cocaine and hurled it out of the window. 'And there was this Great Dane walking around outside and that fucking dog sniffed the lot,' Ozzy recalls. 'Then it started running round the house like a complete lunatic. All night long the dog was doing that. In the end I put on a fur coat and joined it . . .'

Despite the fights, Ozzy and Sharon were head over heels in love and had finally decided to marry. Two things had held them up: firstly, Ozzy's divorce from his first wife Thelma was taking an interminable amount of time and, secondly, the busy tour schedule had not given them sufficient time off to organize anything. Their original plan had been to have a full-on heavy metal wedding back in Britain, with all their friends and families present, as well as groups such as Def Leppard and Motörhead, who by now had become firm friends with Ozzy. In the end, Ozzy decided he could wait no longer. He explains: 'We were having so many problems with my ex-wife trying to stop everything and cause aggravation. It was like half-time in the battle of the freedom to get away from that one, so I said "Right, let's get married now."'

A brief break in July was to provide the perfect opportunity. They had just flown to Hawaii to perform the final two shows of their US tour and realized to their joy that they had five days off before they were due in Japan. 'So in those five days off we thought this is perfect, we'll do it there,' Sharon recalls. They flew from their last gig in Honolulu direct to the tropical paradise island of Maui where the ceremony was to take place. Drummer Tommy Aldridge was best man, and Ozzy typically launched a mammoth forty-eight-hour stag party. Independence Day – 4 July – had been chosen as the date for the wedding. When later asked if he'd been inspired by a love of his adopted country, Ozzy was forced to admit that patriotism had nothing to do with it, he'd simply picked such a memorable date to cut down the chances of getting into trouble for forgetting his wedding anniversary. With Sharon looking stunning in a traditional white dress, and Ozzy donning a white suit, white bow-tie and Hawaiian flower garlands, they made their vows. Proud Sharon said afterwards: 'Might I say that my husband was sober all through the ceremony.' Predictably though it wasn't for long. As Ozzy recalls: 'I made up for it because I had the wedding cake soaked in brandy, nobody would eat it, so we had to liquidize it and drink it!'

The wedding breakfast over, Ozzy wandered out on to the hotel terrace. A traditional Hawaiian band dressed in white trousers and floral shirts were strumming away in the background. Palm trees swayed gently in the breeze on the beach below and couples quietly sipped their cocktails and held hands, entranced by the beauty and romance of the scene. This was as close to paradise as many of them had ever been. Ozzy gazed at the sight before him, briefly considered ordering a cocktail and joining them and then immediately dismissed the thought. It might be his wedding, it might be the most romantic day of his life, but it just wouldn't be a proper celebration without some good old-fashioned rock and roll. With a mischievous grin on his face, Ozzy boldly walked right up on to the stage. The bemused musicians paused for a while as Ozzy explained that he was a musician himself, he had just got married and wanted to celebrate by making some music of his own. The group was persuaded to hand over some of their instruments, which Ozzy promptly distributed amongst his band. Borrowing some garlands to wear around their necks, they then took to the stage where, to the shock of the other guests, they launched into a raucous rendition of a string of Ozzy's favorite Beatles songs. The show ended inevitably with a full-on performance of 'Paranoid'. Ozzy remarked afterwards: 'It was a great wedding, the best wedding I've ever had in my life and I don't want another one because you can't top the one I had. I'm desperately in love with my wife and I swear to God it's the best thing that's ever happened. I'm a very proud husband.'

The couple completed their outstanding tour dates in Japan, honeymooned and returned to America, determined to take a longer rest. But Ozzy found to his shock that, in their absence, Don Arden had booked him a string of further dates in America. To add insult to injury, he'd agreed that the singer would deliver a live album. Epic Records had offered Don a huge amount of money for the tour dates and album and he just couldn't resist. Both Sharon and Ozzy were furious.

They had both long since grown tired of Don's style of management, feeling that if Don had his way Ozzy would be touring permanently, taking only occasional breaks to churn out one sub-standard album after another. Sharon and Ozzy were convinced they could make a better go of things on their own. Reluctantly they agreed to do the live album, but only on the understanding that it would be part of their get-out. After that they would go it alone. Don had wanted a double live album, half Ozzy solo stuff and half old Black Sabbath material. But Sharon insisted that the album would consist entirely of Black Sabbath back catalog material. Two consecutive shows at the Ritz Club in New York were booked for September, where Ozzy and the band would record both nights, playing nothing but Black Sabbath numbers. The album was released under the title *Talk of the Devil*. Twenty years on, it is the only record in Ozzy's entire back catalog that embarrasses him, and, to this day, he is believed to take no royalties from it.

The other part of the get-out deal was that Ozzy would perform some more live American dates. Ozzy was shattered, and reluctant to agree, but Sharon persuaded him, pointing out it was the only way he would ever gain his freedom. Before they began touring, Ozzy and Sharon returned to England for a brief five-day rest, but on the first day back Sharon woke up to find Ozzy gone. He remained missing all day and throughout the next night. Sharon was out of her mind with worry. Ozzy had been at his wit's end when they'd returned to England. He was exhausted from non-stop touring and too much drug abuse. He was desperately unhappy about the debt he had to pay to Don, and Sharon was terrified that this time he might really have done something stupid. She called the police and, in desperation, had Ozzy registered as a missing person. He failed to show up again the next night and, at her wits' end, Sharon went to bed praying that he would eventually turn up the following morning. Her prayers were answered when she woke the following day to find Ozzy standing shivering at the end of the bed. 'And he's standing there with this horrible green woollen hat pulled down over his ears and he's trembling all over,' she recalls. Sharon's relief quickly turned to anger and she screamed at him, telling him how she'd spent a frantic forty-eight hours worried sick, but Ozzy just mumbled an incoherent reply and stood there looking sheepish. He finally pulled off the hat to reveal a bald head. The pressure of the tour had become so much that he had cracked and one day simply shaved off all his hair. They returned to the States to fulfill their contractual obligation performances, but Ozzy's bald head only served to add to his notoriety. The word quickly spread amongst fans that the rabies injections he'd been given after biting the bat had made his hair fall out, so, to calm things down, Sharon went out and bought a range of wigs for him to wear on stage. Ozzy meanwhile issued an explanation denying that the rabies shots had anything to do with it. The bright stage lights combined with the gels and oils he was using in his hair at the time were making his hair brittle and damaged, he explained. To give it a chance to recover, he just shaved it off. Far better the fans believe he had sensitive hair than discover the truth – that their wildman hero actually had sensitive feelings, too.

Tired, drugged and depressed Ozzy ploughed on with the tour. But there was still controversy wherever he went. The day before one show in the American Deep South a preacher went on the local radio to warn his congregation that 'the madman was coming!' One religious group even went so far as to hold a record-burning ceremony to protest about what it saw as the evil of rock and roll. 'One of the albums we're going to be burning tonight is Ozzy Osbourne's *Talk of the Devil*,' said a priest to the waiting crowds. In Chicago, by unfortunate coincidence, Ozzy found himself booked into the same hotel as a bible convention. 'It was like Satan walking into Heaven,' Ozzy recalls. 'It was like a billion rays hitting my face like in *Star Wars*. And next morning there must have been 1,500 religious pamphlets under my door.' Each venue was by now receiving angry phone calls ahead of the show from religious fanatics. 'You'd think by now I would have got used to these fucking maniacs and their pathetic death threats,' Ozzy reasoned, 'But to be perfectly honest my bottle was starting to go at one stage, because things got so bad.' The pressures eventually took their toll, and one night Ozzy collapsed on stage in the middle of a show. There were initially fears he had suffered a heart attack, but it soon emerged that the cause of the problem was sheer exhaustion, compounded by heavy drinking. As soon as the shows ended, Ozzy would down whatever he could get his hands on – wine, whiskey, beer and brandy. But more often than not he would not confine his drinking to the privacy of his hotel room and that's when the trouble would start. 'I go off the rails,' he admitted. 'I am a lunatic. The pressure of work, the pressure, everyone has a stop valve, and I don't have one.'

Ozzy's nerves were shattered and, a few weeks' later, things came to a head again. Flamboyant Don Costas had recently joined the tour as bass guitarist. His reputation as a live performer was almost unrivalled; he would appear on stage with a cheese grater attached to his guitar and would frequently attack the stage sets with his bare hands or a pickax. For a while he was Ozzy's hero, but Ozzy was growing increasingly irritated and bored by Costas's outlandish behavior. He felt there was only room for one showman on stage. It was his tour and he'd built up the support with many years of hard work, so Costas should tone things down a little. Sitting at the back of the tour bus together one night after a show, Ozzy decided to let Don know exactly how he felt. Suddenly all hell broke loose and Don staggered down the aisle covered in blood, with his nose wrecked. 'Ozzy had given him the old Birmingham sandwich – he'd head-butted Don and broken his nose,' recalls Sharon. The next day an apologetic Ozzy handed over $5,000 (£3,450) for Don to get his nose fixed in a private Los Angeles clinic and the tour limped on, Ozzy counting down the days, desperate for the tour to end, desperate for his freedom.

Don Arden was not going to give up Ozzy without a fight, though, and was furious that his daughter wanted to manage him single-handed. Finally, to wrench themselves away, she reluctantly agreed to buy out Ozzy's management contract for $1.5 million (£1 million). She could not forgive her father for the way he had behaved and broke off all contact with him there and then. In the mid-1980s Don faced trial for false imprisonment and blackmail of business associates. He was acquitted, but his son David was found guilty of the same charge, and jailed. Sharon says: 'The best lesson I ever had was watching him fuck his business up. He taught me everything not to do. My father's never even seen any of my three kids and as far as I'm concerned he never will.' True to her word, Sharon even insisted that she and Ozzy rewrote their wills after their children were born, to ensure that, in the event of their deaths. Don and his wife Hope would have nothing to do with bringing up the children. Ozzy understood her anger. 'They were very unfair to me, I worked my backside off to keep their company going and they didn't generate anything back in to me,' he says. 'Although it's my father-in-law I have no respect for those people because they have no respect for me or their daughter.' It was a feud that was to last almost two decades, father and daughter being reconciled only in November 2001.

As the tour ended, Sharon promised Ozzy a lengthy break from the road and time out to record his first studio album in two and a half years. She understood her star performer far better than any suit in a large office could ever do. She loved him and, caring about his health recognized that he needed a proper rest. But Sharon was also a shrewd businesswoman. She knew that after the disappointment of the live album the fans would be desperate for some fresh Ozzy material. If he had a break and re-charged his batteries he would be able to deliver a new album that was fresh and full of the traditional Ozzy spark and originality. An album that would sell, and keep Ozzy at the top.

To many in the music industry, Sharon and Ozzy were the odd couple. In the early 1980s she showed scant interest in the fashions of the day and many dismissed her as little more than a suburban housewife. 'People would openly say "You and Ozzy won't last,"' she remembers. 'They expected him to have a big-titted blonde trophy wife and he'd got me, a short, fat, hairy, half-Jew. I had a lot to fight against.' But, behind the mumsy frocks, Sharon was fast forging a reputation as one of the most driven managers in the music business. 'I'm pretty reasonable,' she once explained. 'If I were a man, I'd just be seen as this great toughie businessman. I'm a woman, so men say "Oh, she's a bitch."'

Ozzy had never met a woman quite like her before and he was besotted. He'd loved his first wife, but their lives had been so different that, in the end, it was impossible for them to get along. He'd made the most of the willing groupies on the road during his time, but one-night stands with anonymous women were never really his scene and he was often sickened by how cheap it made him feel. Sharon was altogether different. Sexy, ballsy and bright, she gave as good as she got. Like Ozzy, she swore like a trooper and loved to laugh at the absurdities of life. She understood the pop business and Ozzy's appeal perfectly and was a tough negotiator who would fight fiercely for her man in the boardroom. He trusted her and, although he would complain, deep down he was more than happy to follow her lead. 'My wife is the ruler of the roost, she tells me what to do most of the time,' he once conceded. 'A lot of people think Ozzy is the man, but it's a true old saying that behind every great man is a great woman and I've got the greatest woman in the world working for me. It's fabulous.'

Pop commentator Rick Sky met Ozzy and Sharon on several occasions in the early to mid 80s during his time working for British newspapers the *Sun* and the *Daily Star*. The time Sky spent with them convinced him that they are the perfect double act. 'Sharon is very forceful and she understands Ozzy completely,' he says. 'They are opposites in many ways, but she's the daughter of Don Arden who was a fairly hot-headed businessman with a ferocious temper so she's always been used to that and maybe she sees Ozzy as a challenge. But they certainly have a brilliant relationship and they genuinely, genuinely adore each other.

'I remember he used to put on a baby voice and, with this thick Birmingham accent, he'd say "Ozzy's been a bad, bad boy and Shaz is very upset with Ozzy. Ozzy went out drinking last night and Shaz found out." He sounded like something from *Andy Pandy*, a children's TV program in Britain in the 50s. He's like a naughty boy who is repentant, but not really, and she's like his mother, his wife and his manager all rolled into one. They're a perfect couple in that way.'

And Sharon's undoubted influence on his life and career is something that Ozzy, too, is happy to acknowledge. 'My wife is the most incredible woman I've ever met in my life,' he says simply. 'Because unlike the normal housewife who doesn't know about much, she knows more about things in my opinion than ninety per cent of these politicians know. She doesn't think and talk about it, she gets off her backside and does it, which is great.'

chapter seven

Family Matters

❝ *My kids never had to adjust. They were born into this dysfunctional world of mine. It's more difficult for them to understand people with a day job.* ❞

IT WAS ONE of the proudest moments of his life. He'd had hit records; he'd sold millions of albums and made and lost a fortune. He'd slept with more women that he could remember and appeared on the front cover of magazines around the globe. If he'd been capable of remembering them, he could have named a thousand and one memorable moments, but nothing had ever touched Ozzy quite like this. The birth of his and Sharon's first child on 2 September 1983, had reduced the supposed hard man of rock to tears. For once, the waiting crowds meant nothing– all he wanted right now was to be with his wife and newborn baby.

Away from the crowds, Ozzy was a devoted family man. He had loved his two children from his first marriage and had been devastated when he broke up from their mother. Now happily married to Sharon, he had a second chance of family happiness and he just couldn't believe his luck. Baby Aimee Rachel Osbourne was just an hour old. Ozzy had hugged Sharon and told her how proud he was of her a hundred times and now his new daughter, wrapped in a simple white shawl, had been placed in his arms for the first time. Standing at Sharon's bedside, with tears of joy and pride pouring down his cheeks, he gently stroked Aimee's cheek, held her tiny fingers and softly whispered how much he would always love her. He would never leave her and Sharon, he promised. He would always be there for them and he would do everything in his power to make them happy. Sharon smiled up at her husband. This was the Ozzy the world never saw. The reason she loved him, the reason she could put up with his wild, uncontrollable ways. Gently, she reminded him that there was a crowd outside, journalists and fans waiting to hear the happy news. Ozzy dried his eyes, gave them both one last kiss, and reluctantly headed out of the door. It would only take a second, he promised, he would be back as quickly as he could.

There was a huge cheer as Ozzy emerged from the hospital doors. Was he there for the birth? a reporter enquired as the crowd jostled to get closer. Ozzy paused, Should he tell them the truth? Should he talk about his tears, his pride and the uncontrollable surge of love he felt when he held his newborn daughter for the first time? Suddenly his eyes lit up and the old demonic grin returned to his lips. Tell the truth, and wreck his hard-earned reputation as the Prince of Darkness? Of course not. Better to tell them that he'd been tempted to bite the head off his daughter than admit she'd actually reduced him to tears. Ozzy launched into a virtuoso performance. 'Was I fucking there?' he replied. 'Was I fucking ever! Fuck me! They tell you all about being there to hold the old lady's hand and help her breathe and all that shit and then you get there and it's like a scene from *The Exorcist*! Blood and fucking guts everywhere! The doctors were on about giving her drugs for the pain, I was like, fuck that, give 'em to me!'

Just a few moments earlier at Sharon's side, Ozzy had been genuinely emotional, a devoted new dad, who just couldn't contain his feelings. But in front of a crowd he was instantly transformed into Ozzy the showman. His audience didn't expect tears and gentleness from the man who had bitten the head off a bat; they wanted the wild and controversial Ozzy they had known and loved for years. And Ozzy, as ever, delivered.

In many ways, the birth of baby Aimee changed Ozzy forever. From that day on, he and Sharon shared something greater than their marriage vows and their professional relationship. They had a family. Ozzy doted on Aimee. Doctors had tried to tame him. He'd tried to tame himself with drugs and drink, and Sharon had lost count of the different tactics she'd tried to get him to calm down. But all of a sudden, without effort, this gurgling, helpless little girl had done it. Like many men who seem wild and uncontrollable, Ozzy was actually extremely at ease with children. Maybe he felt they understood him better, maybe he simply felt he was on their wavelength – by his own admission he had never grown up – but with baby Aimee in his arms, he was as happy as it was possible to be.

Ozzy, however, was wracked with guilt about the fact that he rarely saw his children from his first marriage. He was now based almost entirely in Los Angeles, but his children remained with their mother back in Britain. His adopted son Elliot was now seventeen, his daughter Jessica Starshine was eleven and his youngest son Louis was now eight. In an interview just before Aimee was born, he told excitedly how Jessica had started tap dancing and how he had persuaded his ex-wife to let him borrow little Louis to feature alongside him on the front cover of his album *Diary of A Madman.* 'I have one daughter, one son, and an adopted son, from that first marriage, but my prodigy, my next life, is my Bombins,' he said proudly. 'He's my double. His name's Louis, but I call him Bombins. Bombins is my next me.' Typically, Ozzy had dreamt up the name Bombins one day after growing tired of using the boy's real name. His ex-wife reluctantly agreed to allow Louis to answer to the name, but when Ozzy told her that he was also bored with Jessica's name and wanted to start calling her Burt Reynolds instead, she put her foot down firmly. Ozzy reluctantly backed down, but was undeterred. Jessica was too conventional a name for a daughter of the famous Ozzy Osbourne, he reasoned.

He might not be able to get away with Burt Reynolds, but he was damned if he would be beaten, and the minute his wife was out of earshot he told the giggling little girl that his new secret name for her was now Sid.

With his first family thousands of miles away, Ozzy told Sharon that he would like to have a bigger family with her. Although he didn't particularly get on with most of his brothers and sisters, Ozzy had come from a large family and felt children benefited from growing up with others of their own age around them. Luckily, Sharon agreed. Although she had grown estranged from her brother David in recent years, she had fond memories of their childhood together back in England. Within three months Sharon was pregnant again and their second child, Kelly Osbourne, was born on October 27, 1984.

Ozzy was overjoyed. 'My kids mean more to me than anything else in this poxy world,' he said. 'That's all I really care about, when it comes right down to it. The touring is going to have to be fitted in around whatever plans I make with my family these days. I certainly don't want to spend another three years on the road doing nothing but touring.' Ozzy was determined to do his very best to be a good, if rather unconventional, dad. Two years earlier, on a visit to Britain, he'd taught his then fifteen-year-old son Elliot to smoke marijuana, telling him that he would rather he smoked dope than cigarettes. Tobacco is the subtlest drug of all, he warned, but marijuana is safer because it is physically impossible to smoke as much dope in a day as tobacco. 'Being a parent is harder than being a rock 'n' roll singer on the road,' Ozzy once admitted. 'I mean cos any second your kid will run through the door with a sixteen-inch nail sticking through his head, going "Daddy, I just got hit with a 4×2!" And you know, it's like "What?!"'

When the children were young, parenting was easy enough. Ozzy could cope with picking the kids up when they fell over, playing the fool to keep them amused and even changing the odd diaper. But as the children grew older, he found it harder and harder to live up to the mental picture of a good dad he carried round in his head. To Ozzy, a good dad was someone calm and responsible, someone who could lead by example. Someone, in fact, not a bit like himself. 'The hardest job in the world is to be a parent,' he conceded. 'You try to lead them up the right path. But who am I to lead anybody up any fucking path? How can I give out the rules when I'm worse than them most of the time? When they've seen me coming home in police cars, in fucking ambulances, in straitjackets and chains?'

But on that magical day when Aimee was born in September 1983, the full realization of the demands of being a full-time dad to his three young children was yet to come. He and Sharon were still trying to strike a balance between a punishing work schedule and maintaining his health and sanity.

Ozzy had taken the much-needed break that Sharon had used as a carrot to see him through the last remaining dates of his last tour. They'd spent some time together, he'd caught up on some sleep and then he'd launched himself headlong with renewed enthusiasm and energy into the recording of his third solo studio album, *Bark At The Moon*. The title for the album came from a joke Ozzy used to tell in which the punch line was 'Eat shit and bark at the moon.' He had originally contemplated making the album at Nassau's Compass Point Studio, a tropical beauty spot that was fast becoming the 'in'-recording place amongst rock stars in the know. But Ozzy – quite sensibly for once – reasoned that such a paradise location could prove distracting for both himself and the band. What's more, if he were to produce an album that would wow both his critics and his expectant fans, he needed the stability of a familiar place. Ozzy flew to England and took the band back to Ridge Farm Studios in Surrey to set about his work. The band worked hard, Ozzy a bag of edgy nerves. The songs completed, he decided he didn't like the drum sound and ordered a last minute re-mix of the entire album at a New York studio. When he was finally satisfied, the album was scheduled for worldwide release on 2 December 1983. But first there was a bit of dressing up to do . . .

For the album's front cover and accompanying video, Ozzy had decided to turn himself into a were-wolf. He called in a team of make-up artists headed by American Greg Cannon, who had created the stunning visual effects on *An American Werewolf in London*. The video was going to cost more than $72,500 (£50,000) – each hair on his head and body had to be glued individually and the wig alone would be $2,900 (£2,000) – but Ozzy figured it would be worth it. Realizing there was good publicity to be made out of such a spectacle, he invited British *Daily Star* photographer Ken Lennox round to the studios to witness the incredible transformation. 'It took a team of make-up artists six hours to get this horrific werewolf look. You'd think Ozzy would be tearing his hair out but he was actually incredibly patient while they did their work,' he recalls. Then just before filming was due to start, Sharon arrived with baby Aimee, who was just three weeks old. For Ozzy it was the perfect opportunity to live up to his wild man reputation, and he told the shocked make-up team that he was hoping he'd soon be able to persuade Sharon to start feeding baby Aimee with bat's blood instead of 'filthy milk'. Photographer Ken immediately spotted the perfect photo opportunity and asked Ozzy to pick up the baby and pose with her. Ozzy jumped at the idea. 'He told me that when his daughter was older she'd look back at the picture and say he was better looking now than when he was younger!' recalls Ken. 'But I remember that behind the jokes he was very careful with her. He was worried that the long fingernail extensions he was wearing might scratch her, so he asked Sharon to place her in his arms, rather than pick her up himself.'

The startling image of beauty and the beast was published around the world and the accompanying single 'Bark At The Moon' reached Number Twenty-One in the British charts – his biggest solo success so far. Predictably, when the album was released a month later, it soared up the charts. Ozzy was back. Immediately, he launched into a British tour. The crowds flocked back as if he'd never been away, and he was invited to appear on Britain's leading pop TV show, *Top of the Pops*. It was his first solo appearance on the program, but, to his disappointment, he was banned from wearing the full werewolf costume as he'd planned, because TV producers felt it would scare the show's younger viewers.

In January 1984 Ozzy returned to the States to kick off his biggest US tour to date. Having attracted more publicity than she could have imagined on the last two tours, Sharon was determined that things would be different this time around. Now she wanted Ozzy to be judged for his music alone, not for his off-stage antics or the behavior of the crowd. Furthermore, she didn't want him to be distracted by wild partying. Ozzy's drugs intake was as immense as ever. To try to keep him as clean as possible, she slapped a ban on all pre-show drinking, drugs and even sex for the entire band and crew. Anyone caught breaking the rules would either be sacked or have their pay docked. It was a tough rule, but Ozzy was happy to go along with it. For the first time in his career, it was he and his wife who were laying down the law, not the record company or an outside manager. After all the bad experiences they'd been through, Ozzy and Sharon knew exactly how they wanted things done. Rule number one was that Ozzy would pay his band members well above the going rate. Rule number two was that you don't mess with Ozzy. There were no more rules. Ozzy explained once: 'We're not heavy, but the thing is if you're so easygoing with people they think you're a jerk. You get these upstarts who come in and think they know it all, but if people try to pull the wool over our eyes, we turn round and we just don't give them a second chance, if they screw us, they're fired.'

For their support act, Ozzy and Sharon had booked Mötley Crüe. The band was fast developing a reputation as a serious heavy rock group and even more serious party animals. If Sharon had any plans for keeping Ozzy's nose clean, then Mötley Crüe would blow them apart. She said afterwards: 'They're all a great bunch of guys. And at the same time it's not their fault that Ozzy's got a drink and drugs problem. But at times of course, on that tour, them and Ozzy together were a horrendous problem.'

A catalog of incidents ensued:

In Memphis, Tennessee, Ozzy was arrested 'staggering drunk' at 12.30 am and thrown in a cell. He was released at 5.30 am when he had partially sobered up.

In Jacksonville, Florida, as a dare, Ozzy did the whole show in stockings and suspenders, a dress and bra. The outraged City Fathers banned him from ever appearing on stage in the town again.

A few days later, while still in Florida, Ozzy was arrested for peeing on a pavement. He offered to lick it up but the arresting officer was not amused, and he was taken to court and fined.

Sharon may have toned down his stage show slightly, but there was little she could do to rein in Ozzy's unique sense of humor.

A British photographer based in New York at that time recalls that even off duty Ozzy was always playing the clown. The photographer had been dispatched by his newspaper to meet Ozzy during a brief break in the tour at his home in LA. He was unsure how to get from the airport to Ozzy's house, so the singer generously offered to drive to the airport and pick him up. 'I walked out into the airport car park with Ozzy who insisted on carrying my bags. The place was full of these huge expensive cars, but Ozzy walked up to this mangled wreck and proudly pointed out the bumper sticker, which read 'My Other Car Went Up My Nose'. I'd asked him to be careful with the bags as they contained some very expensive camera equipment, but of course by the time we'd reached the car he'd forgotten and he opened up the boot and just threw them inside!' the photographer recalls. 'The place was crawling with police and Ozzy, wearing dark glasses and dressed entirely in black, had caught their eye. I was a bit worried and when we got inside the car I asked him if he'd noticed that all the policemen were staring at him rather menacingly. "Yeah," he said, "But don't worry, I caught their eye and gave them a wink so they'll be fine." "Ozzy", I pointed out, "you're wearing sunglasses."' When they reached Ozzy's house the photographer commented that Ozzy had lost a lot of weight and was looking in good shape. Ozzy told him that it was all down to the coke diet. 'What? Diet Coke?' the photographer asked innocently. 'No, cocaine, you prat!' replied Ozzy, roaring with laughter.

But even when he was doing his best to avoid the headlines, trouble seemed to find Ozzy. During a break in the US tour, Ozzy had flown to Britain to record a video for what was to be his next single, 'So Tired'. During the video a mirror was to appear to explode in front of his face. It should have been sugar-glass, but by mistake real glass was used, and shards of sharp glass were blasted into Ozzy's throat. He was rushed to hospital and, after being cleaned up, was released to fly home on Concorde, but pressure in the cabin forced more fragments of glass deeper into his throat, causing him agonizing pain. The pilot radioed ahead and an ambulance was waiting on the tarmac in New York. Ozzy was rushed to the Mount Sinai hospital, where surgeons carried out a long and delicate operation to remove the glass. There was no permanent damage to his vocal chords, but the injuries were bad enough to force him to postpone eight US shows.

In the early summer of 1984, with the US tour over, Ozzy flew direct to Tokyo for his first-ever solo tour of Japan. The press, naturally, were out in force. Most of them had been sent by their Editors to find as many scandalous stories as they could about the wild man of rock, but all of them returned bowled over by the cheeky Birmingham rocker. To his surprise, a journalist on Britain's *Observer* newspaper found himself in charge of Ozzy's baby daughter Aimee for the tour. Years later, when they met up again, the journalist greeted Ozzy with a hug and asked him: 'Do you remember when we were in Tokyo and you assigned me the task of wheeling your nine-month-old daughter in a pram all around the city?' 'No,' replied Ozzy. 'I was pissed at the time. But I do remember you. You were a bit of a prat, weren't you?' However, a British photographer who covered the same tour remembers being surprised by the difference between Ozzy's stage persona and his real self. He says: 'You expect to meet this loud lunatic. You can see that side of him is there and he does go through the motions, but it's like meeting an actor who has played the part of a crazy bad guy. Underneath there's actually a lot more to him and, if anything, he's actually slightly shy. He's intelligent and articulate and incredibly self-deprecating and most of the time he's actually very quietly spoken.'

In August 1984 Ozzy briefly returned to Britain to play the famous rock festival at Castle Donington. The show was a popular annual event in the British

Summer festival calendar, and was a showcase for both established and up-and-coming metal and rock bands. It was his first festival appearance for many years and the crowd loved it. The livers and intestines were by now a thing of the past, instead fans hurled bottles at the stage. Ozzy, who'd clearly taken a drink before stepping on stage, proceeded to live up to his reputation by drinking the contents of each and every bottle, however unappetizing they might seem. After the show, Ozzy insisted on taking his entourage for a meal at the local Indian restaurant. The restaurant had been warned in advance that the singer was on his way and had rushed around trying to spruce up the place in honor of their famous visitor. They needn't have bothered, because when the group arrived no one gave a second glance at the décor and barely even looked at the menu. Instead, everyone was mesmerized by Ozzy, who had turned up for the meal wearing a yellow and white floral maternity dress that belonged to his wife. Donington, however, was to be his last show for some time under the influence of drink.

If Ozzy wanted to live up to his mental picture of a perfect dad, it was time for him to make some major changes in his life. He and Sharon were about to move to Palm Springs. They would stay there for a short time while they made the arrangements to buy a house in London. They both wanted a fresh start, Ozzy especially. At thirty-six, he was no longer enjoying the drink and drug-fuelled parties. The highs weren't as high these days and the hangovers were taking longer and longer to subside.

On 28 October 1984 – the day after Kelly's birth – in a decision that shocked himself as much as Sharon, he announced that he would be checking in to the Betty Ford Clinic, hidden away high in the mountains at Rancho Mirage above Palm Springs. He'd been there once before. Shortly before he married Sharon, she insisted he book in, in order to learn to 'drink like a gentleman'. Ozzy left the clinic as soon as possible, telling anyone who would listen that it had all been a huge misunderstanding and that he'd only agreed to go in the first place because he assumed the place had a bar and would set about educating him how to drink the same amounts without throwing up. The second visit to the Clinic was his own decision, and this time he was deadly serious. He wanted to rid himself of his dependency on alcohol and cocaine once and for all. The world-famous Betty Ford Clinic had helped a whole host of celebrities clean up their act and Ozzy reckoned they were just the people to help him. He signed up for a four-and-a-half month treatment, which initially involved a costly $7,250 (£5,000) six weeks stay as a boarder. 'I was killing myself out on the road in America for nearly four years and I just had to go somewhere and get help,' Ozzy said simply.

Initially, though, it seemed as if Ozzy was going to treat the course with the same irreverence with which he treated everything in his life. He found himself sharing a room with a junkie struggling to come off drugs. At night the poor man would lie in his bed groaning with the agony of his addiction, but Ozzy, despite having been through problems of his own, had little sympathy for him. Far from it, threatening to punch the man if he did not keep quiet.

Every day at the clinic would start in the same way, with exercise classes, followed by group therapy sessions, in which individual members would recount what had driven them to drink or drugs in the first place. There would then be films showing people indulging their excesses and generally wrecking the lives of themselves and those around them. A favorite film with the staff was the salutary story of an addict who had gone along to a party with his wife, then immediately got drunk on all the free drink and then sneaked off to the bathroom for a line of cocaine. Everything begins to fall apart in his life and, eventually, his wife leaves him taking their children with her. The only problem was that Ozzy found the film hilarious. 'That bastard tickled me,' admitted Ozzy with a laugh afterwards. 'He was having such a good time while it was all going on around him. I started cheering and clapping every time he chucked one back or sneaked off to take another line. That's when they banned me from attending the film classes. I was having too much of a good time watching them!'

Deep down, however, Ozzy was actually taking the course seriously, sitting down every night and writing letters to his friends in the music business, urging them to follow in his footsteps and check themselves in. And when the stay was over, it was a different Ozzy who emerged. He was fitter, toned and tanned and, for the first time since he was a child, his eyes and skin glistened with health. Sharon was delighted. She'd taken to telling interviewers that her sex life was a disaster because Ozzy usually couldn't even make it upstairs and was relieved to have her husband back in shape again. She and Ozzy and the two children saw in the New Year with glasses of Diet Coke in their hands – Ozzy's first sober New Year's for more than a decade. The following month they were moving to England to start afresh, and by February, Sharon was pregnant again. Life for the Osbournes was looking good.

In January 1985 Ozzy decided to carry out first official public performance since his much publicized clean-up, flying to Rio de Janeiro with Sharon to appear at the first–ever Rock in Rio festival. His plan to stop touring and stay at home to bring up his kids was abandoned. From now on, the children would go everywhere with him. 'Circus folk bring their children up that way, so why not us?' he explained. He may not have been drinking, but Ozzy had lost none of his sense of fun and, after arriving at Rio's Copacabana Palace Hotel, he headed straight for the hotel restaurant for a spot of lunch. He loudly ordered chicken curry, telling the confused waiter, 'And don't forget to leave the head on!' But some things had changed and that night rock musicians and journalists alike watched open-mouthed with disbelief as Ozzy walked into the hotel's packed bar and ordered two mineral waters with ice.

Unfortunately, Ozzy's new sober existence wasn't to be all plain sailing. After Rio, Ozzy flew back to Britain. Sharon and Ozzy were living in a beautiful rented house off Berkeley Square, one of London's most exclusive addresses, while their new house in the smart suburb of Hampstead was refurbished. While Sharon looked after the children and supervised the work on the house, Ozzy started work on his new album *The Ultimate Sin*. But he soon discovered that once back in his old routines he was sorely tempted to take up where he had left off. He explained: 'When you know you really need a drink, that's when you realize you're actually addicted, you can't allow yourself one even. It's what makes alcoholism such a hard fucker to beat; it's so completely socially acceptable, everybody in the world drinks.' Every now and then, out of boredom, he would take a drink, but when he did, the hangovers were worse than ever and he would suffer crippling stomach pains. He would also sink into a deep depression over his lack of self-control. 'One beer and I end up drinking a bottle of vodka, insulting everybody and going to bed,' he said one day, with evident self-disgust.

Since Ozzy had left Black Sabbath back in 1978, the band had continued to tour and produce albums. There had been various line-ups but Tony Iommi had held things together and, while they weren't making as many headlines without their flamboyant frontman, they were certainly still pleasing the record-buying public. In every interview in the intervening seven years,

Ozzy was always asked the inevitable question: 'Will you ever get back together again?' The answer was always a resounding no. But in the early summer of 1985, something happened to make Ozzy finally change his mind. A phone call out of the blue from Terry 'Geezer' Butler set the ball rolling. An Irish singer by the name of Bob Geldof was putting together a charity concert for Ethiopia called Live Aid. It was to be the largest single pop event in history and Black Sabbath had been asked to re-form with the original line-up to play on the same bill as some of the biggest names in pop and rock. To Geezer's surprise, Ozzy agreed. Tony was already in on the plan and Ozzy agreed to call drummer Bill Ward. The event was scheduled to take place at two venues – Wembley in London and Philadelphia – on 13 July and Sabbath would perform three numbers, 'Paranoid', 'Children of the Grave' and 'Iron Man'. The band was booked to play the American end and Ozzy and Sharon decided to travel from England to the States in style on the luxurious *QEII* ocean cruiser. The journey served to furnish Ozzy with a hundred and one hilarious anecdotes for the waiting press at the other end. 'I'll never go on it again, it drove me nuts. Bingo and ballroom dancing, that's all it was.' When a journalist asked how he had managed to keep himself amused during all those days at sea, he deadpanned, 'I became great at crossword puzzles.' It was clearly not what the reporter was expecting. He'd be lucky to get a single column story with an anecdote like that, certainly not the front page he was hoping for. Ozzy looked at his disappointed face and relented. 'But it's mainly just a load of old fuckers sitting around in wheelchairs,' he went on. 'The only real amusement you could get would be having a game seeing who could push the wheelchairs furthest over the side.' Ozzy's audience expected him to live up to his crazy reputation. He'd always given them what they wanted. Why stop now?

The Live Aid shows went ahead watched by a world-wide television audience of billions. Ozzy didn't disappoint. In a huge purple and gold cloak, he strutted and strode around the stage urging the crowd to go crazy. They obeyed the command to the letter and when he eventually left the stage, it was with the screams of the audience ringing in his ears.

Live Aid had been an important landmark for Ozzy, a demonstration to the music world that at the age of thirty-six he could still compete with men ten years his junior. A demonstration that he was still up there with the best. What's more he was now the proud father of another child – baby Jack, born on 8 November. The year was ending on a high and Ozzy finally seemed to be on top of the world. His drinking was under control, he was still in demand with the fans and he had an idyllic home life, devoted wife and three kids. For the first time ever, he seemed to have reached a balance in his life. Not for the first time, he was to be proved terribly wrong.

chapter eight

Suicide Solution?

> ❛ I'm the guy kids love and parents hate.
> When you've achieved that, you've achieved a goal. ❜

THE CORONER SWALLOWED HARD as he entered the room. He had seen many disturbing sights in his time, but suicides were always the worst. In this case the victim, John McCollum, had shot himself in the head. To add to the tragedy the young man in question was only nineteen. But as the coroner gazed sadly at the life-less body, pondering what torment had driven him to such a desperate act, he spotted something unusual; the boy was still wearing music headphones. Puzzled, he walked across to the stereo in the corner of the room, curious to discover the last sounds the boy had heard before he died. There on the turntable before him was Ozzy Osbourne's song 'Suicide Solution'.

The first Ozzy knew of the tragic event was two years later, in 1986, when he got off a plane at Los Angeles airport to a waiting crowd of reporters. How did he feel, they asked, about being held responsible for the death of one of his teenage fans? How did he feel, they pressed, about being sued by the boy's parents who claimed that Ozzy's lyrics had caused the death? Ozzy was astounded, and drove straight to his lawyer's office, where he discovered to his horror that on 13 January 1986, John's parents, still grief-stricken over the death of their son, had launched a lawsuit against the singer and his record company. They had hired attorney John Anderson who had already stacked up a whole raft of alleged evidence against the singer. Anderson said he had received at least twenty phone calls from parents, indicating that their children had committed suicide not just listening to rock music, but specifically listening to Ozzy Osbourne. Things were beginning to look bleak. But there was even more. The Institute for Bio-Acoustics Research was hired to evaluate the song and found subliminal lyrics that weren't included on the official lyric sheet. The subliminal lyrics, they said, were: 'Why try, why try? Get the gun and try it. Shoot, shoot, shoot', followed by hideous laughter. These lyrics, the Institute alleged, were sung at one and a half times the normal rate of speech and would not be recognized by a first-time listener. They would only be audible if someone played the song over and over again. Furthermore, the analysts found unusual tones in the song, which they said were the result of a special process that used sound waves to influence an individual's mental state, including the rate at which the human brain assimilates information. Their case was that these tones had made John vulnerable to the suggestive lyrics that Ozzy sang.

Condemning Ozzy, John's father Jack said: 'They know what they are putting out. There are people who are out there trying to make money and they have no hesitation to sell your kids down the drain. You see a perfectly normal kid there who doesn't show any signs of depression at all – happy. Then six hours later he's dead. Nobody can explain it. The only thing we know is that he was listening to this music.'

Ozzy was devastated. He was heartbroken that a young fan had shot himself listening to his music, but he could not accept that anyone would hold him personally responsible and his defense was vehement. Firstly, he was adamant that there were no hidden lyrics: 'I swear on my life I never said "get the fucking gun"', he insisted. Secondly, he explained that the lyrics that did exist were not about suicide. The song 'Suicide Solution', which had featured on his first solo album *Blizzard of Ozz*, had been written after the death of former AC/DC singer Bon Scott. Scott had died after drinking heavily and passing out in his car one winter's night. Ozzy said the tragedy had prompted him to write a song warning about the dangers of alcohol. The opening verse began:

> *Wine is fine*
> *But whiskey's quicker*
> *Suicide is slow with liquor*
> *Take a bottle, drain your sorrows*
> *Then it floods away tomorrows.*

The solution he was referring to was alcohol, Ozzy insisted. He was simply suggesting it was a deadly liquid. At the same time, Ozzy's lawyer argued that the First Amendment of the American Constitution meant that Ozzy could, in fact, write about anything he wanted. Furthermore, he said, the additional noises that could be heard were not subliminal but simply Ozzy fooling around on the mixing machine in the studio. It was a sound defense. But it still wasn't going to be easy for Ozzy. The case by now had received so much publicity that more and more parents were coming forward to blame teenage deaths on the influence of heavy metal. A fourteen year-old from Minnesota had committed suicide by shooting himself with a rifle after telling his father he couldn't cope with the pressure of life. Afterwards his mother revealed that his favorite groups were Van Halen, AC/DC, Mötley Crüe, Quiet Riot, Black Sabbath and Ozzy Osbourne. He would also watch MTV all day and then right through the night until six in the morning. The suggestion was clearly that watching back-to-back heavy rock videos had altered his mind. Meanwhile, an Osbourne cassette had been found in a van in which a sixteen-year-old Georgia boy fatally shot himself, and it also emerged that back in 1971, a nurse had committed suicide after listening to Black Sabbath's *Paranoid* album. Even more dramatically, the Canadian Press Wire Service reported that the effects of Ozzy's heavy rock music so influenced a young Canadian that he went out and killed. James Jollimore, twenty, was charged with the first-degree murder of a forty-four year-old woman and her two sons. His friend told the court that Jollimore felt like stabbing people when he heard music such as Ozzy Osbourne's 'Bark at the Moon'. 'Jimmy said that every time he listened to the song he felt strange inside,' he explained. 'He said when he heard it on New Year's Eve he went out and stabbed someone.'

Ozzy had known since the days of Black Sabbath that some of his fans had a fascination with black magic, but as far as he was concerned he had never encouraged it, and the gothic imagery that featured on many of his album covers was just that – imagery. It meant nothing. Similarly, he could not accept that his music could be responsible for the deaths of otherwise sane people. 'Parents have called me and said "When my son died of a drug overdose your record was on the turntable." I can't help that. These people are freaking out anyway and they need a vehicle for their freak outs,' Ozzy insisted. But, despite his public defiance, he was privately saddened and bewildered by what was happening. He was a father himself and, while he sympathized with the parents' pain, he could not understand how a lawsuit would help matters in any way. 'I don't know about you,' he told one interviewer. 'But if I went home tonight and found my kid lying face down in the bath with a suicide note saying "Goodbye Dad, I'm off" and a New Kids on the Block album was playing on his stereo, the last thing on my mind would be suing the group – I'd be grief stricken.'

After a terrible year of wrangling, in which both sides were put under interminable pressures, a California superior judge finally ruled that the lawsuit should be thrown out. There was insufficient evidence to hold Ozzy responsible, and under the First Amendment he was indeed offered protection, the judge decreed. Ozzy was overjoyed, but, to his dismay, discovered that it was not the end of the matter and incredibly the legal case was to rumble on for another six years. Two years later, in 1991, it went to an appeals court, then before a district court judge in Atlanta; while finally, on 1 October, 1992, the Supreme Court upheld the ruling that the First Amendment protected Ozzy against lawsuits that alleged his music encourages suicide. After being finally cleared, Ozzy expressed his immense relief, while insisting that the case should never have been brought in the first place. 'I know in my heart what the fuck I was writing that song about, so I have no guilty conscience about it,' he explained. 'If it was really about suicide, then I would have felt differently. Whether you want to believe it or not, rock 'n' roll is an art form and being an artist I should be able to sing about whatever the fuck I like.'

The whole episode left Ozzy down, but certainly not out, and on his 1988 album *No Rest For The Wicked* he showed exactly what he felt about the whole subliminal lyrics debate by placing a hidden message on the track 'Bloodbath in Paradise'. 'I got so fed up, I did put a stupid fucking message on a track backwards,' Ozzy admitted afterwards. 'It said "Your mother sells whelks in Hull". I had someone come up to me once and say "Hey, man, what's a fucking whelk, man?"' Not everyone, it seems, understood Ozzy's unusual sense of humor.

While the court case continued, Ozzy had pressed ahead with his music. It would have been natural to have kept a low profile during this difficult time: either release nothing at all or ensure that everything he did write was squeaky-clean to prove he wasn't as bad as everyone made out. But Ozzy never had the expected reaction. In February 1986 – just a month after being sued – he released his new album *The Ultimate Sin*. It made Number Eight in the British album charts and

Number Six in America, but Ozzy immediately ran into trouble with the album's original cover, which showed three crucifixes on the top of a hill, and featured a girl wearing no underwear. On a happier note, the album gave him a Number Twenty hit in Britain with the song 'Shot In The Dark'. 'This was my first hit single,' Ozzy exclaimed afterwards. 'I couldn't believe Ozzy Osbourne with a hit single!' He went back on the road again, but the Ultimate Sin tour proved to be an expensive one. Rioting, once again, was the order of the day and after a show at the Meadowlands Sports Complex in New Jersey Ozzy was landed with a bill for $80,000 (£55,170) damages after encouraging fans to go crazy, rip up seats and throw them towards the stage.

Ozzy at this time was slipping in and out of sobriety. His stay at the Betty Ford Clinic had taught him how to resist drink successfully. The problem was that, deep down, Ozzy wasn't sure he really wanted to resist it. He might have felt and looked better while he was on the wagon, he might get into a lot less trouble, but secretly, he believed he was missing out on a whole lot of fun. 'I thought the problem with that lot at the Betty Ford Clinic was that not one of them probably ever took a decent drink in their life,' he admitted later. 'They never knew what it was like to swing around lamp posts in the street at midnight, drunk out of their minds, completely fucked up. But I do.'

To try to avoid temptation, Ozzy would steer clear of all his old haunts, sticking to coffee bars instead. If he ever did go to a bar, his friends would drink soft drinks all night as a mark of respect for his new-found sobriety. Ozzy found the whole experience tedious. He was also unhappy that in compensation for the lack of drink he had started to eat more and was developing a noticeable waistline. He was clearly an unhappy teetotaler, so his friends and family were disappointed, but not entirely surprised, when he began to drink again.

His days at Betty Ford had failed to teach him moderation. Determined to make up for lost time, Ozzy simply picked up exactly where he had left off. But whether it was age, whether it was his months of sobriety, or whether it was simply the fact that his body could no longer cope, he began to suffer monumental hangovers. They made him miserable, but they didn't make him stop. 'I drink and smoke dope, but my biggest habit is fucking drink. I drink like a fucking fool,' he observed. 'If the bombs don't kill me, then alcohol will.'

At the start of 1987 Ozzy was riding high. The *Ultimate Ozzy* video, based on a concert filmed in Kansas the previous year, went gold. Musically it seemed he could not put a foot wrong. So what next? Any other musician riding such a crest of a wave would have been ordered by their record company to capitalize immediately on their success with another sell-out world tour. But Ozzy's management was Sharon. And while he listened to her advice and opinions on every single aspect of his career, one thing she would never be able to do – or would ever want to do – was stifle Ozzy's love of fun. Instead of touring, Ozzy released the much-awaited Randy Rhoads tribute album in honor of his former guitarist, and then accepted the part of a fanatical fundamentalist priest, the Reverend Aaron Gilstrom, in a new horror movie *Trick Or Treat*. Parodying his own experiences, Ozzy's priest believed that evil was spread through rock music and that he was the man to stop it.

By the summer, to the relief of his fans, Ozzy revealed that he was finally ready to tour again. Rock promoters girded their loins and prepared to make a fortune. Ozzy was now one of the biggest-selling stars in the world and could fill the venues of his choice, from London's Wembley Arena to New York's Madison Square Garden. They were clamoring for him in South

America, across Europe and Asia, Japan and China. This could be the biggest rock tour ever. Finally, to a waiting media, Ozzy announced his plans. Firstly, the tour would take place over six weeks, a slightly shorter period than had been expected. Secondly, the entire tour would take place in Britain. The press were agog and began scribbling frantically. This was no longer a story simply for the pop pages; it would make a news story headline. What they hadn't anticipated was the final announcement that would virtually guarantee them the front page splash – Ozzy's tour would kick off – not as expected at Wembley Arena or the prestigious Royal Albert Hall – but at Wormwood Scrubs, London's most notorious jail, home to some of Britain's most hardened criminals and murderers. That concert over, Ozzy and his band would move around the country playing every UK prison possible. The prisoners, Ozzy explained, would be treated to a selection of Ozzy's greatest hits, including 'Paranoid', 'Bark At The Moon' and 'Crazy Train'. But the encore, he added with a grin, would include a song he had never before played live, a heavy metal version of one of his favorite Elvis songs – 'Jailhouse Rock'.

In 1988 Ozzy released another new album, *No Rest for the Wicked*, which reached Number Twenty-three in Britain and Number Thirteen in the US, and the following March Ozzy enjoyed further success with the single 'Close My Eyes Forever' a duet with Lita Ford, which became a Top Ten US hit. On the surface, it seemed that things had finally settled down for Ozzy. He had drastically reduced his drug-taking, he had a successful recording career – every record he produced these days was an automatic hit – and he had a wonderful wife and three children he adored. But Ozzy had not yet been able to tame the one demon that still haunted him – drink. Frequently, he would disappear on 'lost weekends', where he would leave home for a drink on Thursday night and not return home until the following Wednesday, in a dreadful state. 'My first marriage had been blown out by alcohol and drugs and I was doing a good job on the second one too,' he admits. 'Sharon dealt with it by not saying anything. It was worse than a bollocking. She'd just go "Come on kids, we're out of here."'

Even Ozzy began to think he was going too far. But even Ozzy could not have predicted quite how far he would actually end up going. In August, he had been invited to Russia to play in the Moscow Peace Festival alongside such other heavy metal greats as Bon Jovi, Mötley Crüe and the Scorpions. Although the event had been staged to raise money for people with drink and drug problems, Ozzy was presented afterwards with a case of Russian vodka. Back home in Britain the following Saturday, his daughter Aimee celebrated her sixth birthday. Sharon and Ozzy had decided to mark the day with a quiet family dinner at home. Unfortunately, Ozzy also chose to mark the event by toasting his daughter with a glass of Russian vodka. And once he'd opened one bottle he couldn't stop. 'It was amazing,' he admitted afterwards. 'All these little miniatures of different flavored vodkas. I couldn't wait to get my hands on it.' The case also contained four full-sized bottles of vodka, which, after he'd polished off the miniatures, Ozzy proceeded to down, too. As he got drunker, he got wilder and wilder and Sharon became increasingly frightened. She had seen her husband in terrible states before through too much drink, but this was different. 'It sent him crazy,' she recalls. 'He really did go mad. It was terrifying. I mean, me and my old man have had fist fights before, we've broken up rooms and all that, you know. But never anything like this.' At one point Ozzy, by now wild-eyed and virtually incoherent, grabbed his wife by the throat and started choking her. When Sharon heard the chilling words 'we've decided that you've got to go' she hit the panic button on the house alarm, alerting the police. The police roared up and bundled a screaming and kicking Ozzy into a police car and took him away. The next morning, he awoke in a cell at Amersham police station to the news that he had been arrested for the attempted murder of his wife. Ozzy quipped: 'But I can't have, I was in a Chinese restaurant five minutes ago!' But this time it was no laughing matter. This time, Ozzy's jokes and excuses would not be enough. This time, he was in serious trouble.

On the Monday morning Ozzy appeared in court charged with attempted murder. He was devastated. He genuinely couldn't remember a thing about Saturday night, but he couldn't believe that, however much he'd drunk, he would ever want to kill Sharon. She was the most important person in his life, the person who had saved him, rescued his career and given him hope. He couldn't imagine life without her, let alone wanting to murder her. His plea was to be one of temporary insanity. Sharon didn't want to press charges, and he hoped that the court would accept that he must have been momentarily deranged. Fortunately it did and at Sharon's suggestion, instead of jail, the judge ruled that Ozzy should be sent to Huntercombe Manor, an expensive rehabilitation center in Buckinghamshire. He would stay there for three months, before being brought back before the courts for further assessment. The court order further prohibited him from going anywhere near his family during that time. Ozzy was crushed, but he had no choice but to accept the ruling. He had come so close to being sent away for life and to losing everything he held dear. He might yet lose Sharon and the children, he realized, but if for once he did as he was told, there was just a chance that he might be able to save both himself and what remained of his marriage. To show how sorry he was, Ozzy decided it was time for a grand gesture. He briefly considered sending Sharon flowers or chocolates, but dismissed them as too obvious; he wasn't allowed out to buy her jewelry, and drink would be inappropriate in the circumstances. Instead, Ozzy decided to send Sharon one of the things he held most dear in his life – his hair. Borrowing a pair of scissors he chopped it all off, put it in a box with a note simply saying 'Sorry' and sent it off to her. On opening the gift Sharon, not surprisingly, decided that Ozzy really was in the best place possible right now. The ruling preventing him from contacting his family remained in force throughout his stay, but after a time Ozzy was eventually allowed visits from his children Aimee, Kelly and Jack, by now aged six, five and four. Later, Ozzy revealed: 'They kept asking me "Why are you here, Daddy?" I didn't know what to tell them. It nearly broke my fucking heart waving goodbye to them as they all drove off.'

When his three months were up, Ozzy returned to the court to be told, to his great relief, that it was felt that he had made sufficient progress to be allowed out. More importantly, Sharon was willing to take him back home. Showing a remarkable sense of forgiveness, she explained: 'He was totally insane from all the drink and drugs he was doing, and well, these things happen.' She had gone so far as to have divorce papers drawn up while he was inside, but realized she still loved him, and just could not go through with it. Ozzy, however, was not so easy on himself. Years later he explained: 'If you go out for a drink, you go out for a drink. You don't think: "I'll have a few pints. I'll piss up this shrine. I'm going to punch this copper in the nose, then I'm going to go home, strangle my wife and fucking throw the dog on the fire." That's not your plan, but you end up doing stupid shit like that. I kind of accept it but I'm not really proud of it. It's not something I'll say to my grandchildren: "You know what I did when I was your age?"'

chapter nine

'Mama, I'm Coming Home'

> ❛ I've come to the conclusion that people don't want to know the truth – that I'm a happily married man with three kids that I absolutely adore, and that what I do is entertain people. I am not fucking Dracula. ❜

OZZY AND SHARON had both received a terrible scare after his attempt to strangle her. They both knew that the stay at Huntercombe Manor hadn't actually cured him of his addictions – he'd been to clinics numerous times before and come home supposedly clean, only to lapse again when he became bored. But the couple hoped the whole sorry experience had at least made him come to his senses. Or as much to his senses as Ozzy ever came . . .

Ozzy spent the following year quietly, by his standards, touring with 'Geezer' Butler, and recording a six-song album *Just Say Ozzy*. Then, in 1991, he took the momentous decision to tackle the root cause of all his problems – his twenty-year battle with the bottle. The strange thing was that this time there was no specific reason. He hadn't killed, bitten, peed on or slept with anything or anybody he shouldn't. He'd simply woken up one morning and decided that he'd had enough of the hangovers, the memory loss and the disappointment of his wife. Things had come to a head after Sharon had gone away with the children to visit friends for a week. 'And I just got pissed out of my fucking face every day, drugs and everything, day and night for a week,' Ozzy recalls. 'On the Friday I felt so fucking awful, that I thought, that's it, I can't do it anymore and I just went cold turkey. I woke up on the Sunday with Sharon holding me down. I'd no idea what had happened.'

With the zeal of a religious convert, Ozzy threw every last bottle of drink out of the house and frantically set about becoming a new man. He bought an exercise bike and, although it was all he could manage to assemble it on the first day, he gradually built up until he was using it for ninety minutes a day. He started a diet, cut out red meat and began visiting a gym. But, typically, a man with such an addictive nature as Ozzy's couldn't do anything by halves: 'My addiction switched to exercise. The natural endorphins kick in and I could go on forever.'

While exercise was giving him a natural high, his mind – for the first time unaltered by drink – was a new toy and he immediately set about using it to great effect. His September single release of that year 'No More Tears', which reached Number Thirty-two in the British charts, was a more thoughtful song than many of its predecessors. The album by the same name similarly marked a change in direction. While his previous releases, both with Black Sabbath and as a solo artist, were dark, out-and-out heavy rock albums, this latest release contained softer ballads, including the poignant love song for Sharon, 'Mama I'm Coming Home'. Mama was his pet name for Sharon and the phrase was one he would say to her on the phone towards the end of a tour. The fans clearly appreciated the new, mellower Ozzy and the album went to Number Seven in the US album charts and Number Thirty-two in Britain. The singer was later to say proudly that it was the first album he had ever made sober.

Drink was one thing however, drugs were still another matter. To celebrate the album's completion, Ozzy and the rest of the band had flown to Las Vegas for a long weekend. Ozzy had bought an ounce of cocaine specially, but had taken it before he even boarded the plane. When he arrived in Vegas, the hangers-on, fair-weather friends, and friends of friends that every rock star attracts swooped. Soon Ozzy found himself being offered cocaine left, right and center. Within hours of landing he found that his pockets were stuffed with packets containing twenty-five grams of the stuff. That was Thursday, and by Sunday Ozzy could take no more. The drugs had long since stopped working, he felt terrible and if he heard one more bell on another one-armed bandit he was convinced he would go crazy. His head swimming, he wandered out of the casino, carrying his remaining stash of cocaine in a plastic shopping bag, and hailed a cab. As the cab pulled up, Ozzy hurled the bag towards the side of the road where it caught on a fence. Immediately he began to panic. His flight wasn't until four in the afternoon and it was only 9am. Perhaps he should have kept some of the cocaine to help him through the intervening seven hours? By throwing it all away like that he was putting himself at risk of a seizure. As the car slowly pulled away Ozzy could see the bag hanging from the fence and leaned forward, intending to ask the driver to stop for a second. Instead, he paused, and summoning up a strength he didn't know he possessed, told him to drive on. 'So the rest of the day I'm having cramps and shit-ting and pissing and puking all day,' Ozzy recalls grimly. His withdrawal symptoms were so bad that Ozzy realized he could never go back down that road. It was to be the last time he ever touched cocaine.

Even without it he managed to get into quite enough trouble anyway. The following month, November 1991, he broke four bones in his foot after performing one of his famous frog jumps during a song. In pain, he struggled through three more shows before infection set in and he was forced to cancel the remaining tour dates. In January of the following year, Ozzy was back with a newly healed foot, ready to hit the road again. If ever proof were needed of his split per-sonality – angel one minute, devil the next – then this was it: on 26 March Ozzy touchingly performed a memorial concert at Long Beach California for his much-missed guitarist, Randy Rhoads, dedicating the proceeds to build a new tomb for his old friend. Just two days later, he was handed a bill for $100,000 (£69,000) for damages caused to the Irvine Meadows stadium in Laguna Hills, California, after inviting the audience to join him on stage. Unlike other rock stars, Ozzy has never discouraged excited fans from leaping up and singing along with him. More sensible performers would keep well away while security ejected them, but Ozzy positively embraced uninvited guests, racing towards them, enveloping them in a huge bear hug and then jumping up and down enthusiastically in time to the music with his arms wrapped round them. That was all he'd really planned at Laguna Hills. It was just that the party had got a little out of hand.

With these concerts out of the way, Ozzy finally rescheduled the cancelled dates from the previous year for the summer of 1992. But to the shock and disbelief of his fans the new shows had been renamed the No More Tours tour. These would be his last live performances ever, Ozzy announced. He was retiring from the music business to spend more time with his family. He had finished for good with the grind of life on the road. At least that was the story . . .

In fact, what had really happened was that Sharon had persuaded Ozzy to quit because she secretly believed he was seriously ill. Since giving up drink and drugs Ozzy had developed a strange limping walk. He had been to see his doctor who had sent him to a bone specialist. He put Ozzy's knee in a brace, but, unable to find the cause of the problem, had referred Ozzy to a neurologist. 'So they sent me off to get a brain scan, a body scan, spinal tap, fucking blood work, everything.' After checking all the test results, the neurologist's grim verdict was that Ozzy might have multiple sclerosis. He broke the news to a devastated Sharon, who decided to keep it from Ozzy. Instead, she simply told her husband that she felt it was time he retired. Ozzy was now forty-three and, although he was slightly bemused by her sudden decision, he went along with it. It was true that he did find touring exhausting, he did miss his kids enormously, his health wasn't great and he trusted Sharon's judgment completely. If she felt he was getting too old to play the Prince of Darkness any longer then he was happy to listen to her.

Ozzy suspected nothing, although he did begin to notice a change in Sharon. Normally tough and cool and the sort of woman who took everything in her stride, Ozzy would now often find her in tears for no apparent reason. And – normally the biggest fan of his exuberant stage performances – she had also taken to asking him not to jump around so much on stage. It was to be some months later before Ozzy was eventually to discover the reason for her behavior. During a meeting with Epic Records in New York, Sharon was asked if Ozzy had received a second opinion about the problems with his leg. She hadn't, so the record company executive promptly organized a consultation with one of the country's leading experts. 'Of course I still know nothing about this, I'm just taking handfuls of different pills and morphine shots, pretending to be in pain when I wasn't, so that the supply wouldn't dry up!' Ozzy recalls with a laugh. After a show in Detroit, Sharon had booked a Lear jet to fly Ozzy straight to the specialist in Boston. Ozzy, by now impatient and angry, told Sharon he was sick of doctors and refused to go, but when she broke down in tears and pleaded with him, Ozzy reluctantly caved in. The specialist asked Ozzy to walk up and down across the room and then told him that he definitely did not have MS. Sharon was overjoyed. Ozzy was simply bemused; he'd never suspected he'd had it in the first place so he just couldn't understand all the fuss. Afterwards, when the two were alone, when Sharon explained exactly what she had been through, exactly what she had taken on her shoulders in order to protect him, Ozzy contemplated yet again just how incredibly lucky he was to have such an extraordinary wife.

Having already announced his retirement, Ozzy and Sharon decided he might as well take the year off anyway, rather than explain the suspected MS attack. They would stick to the story that he was tired of life on the road and missing his family, and go ahead with the No More Tours tour as planned. The tour kicked off in June and promised to be Ozzy's most spectacular live set to date. His band now consisted of talented and flamboyant guitarist Zakk Wylde, who had been with Ozzy for four years, having been plucked from the obscurity of a New Jersey bar when he was just nineteen; drummer Randy Castillo, another Ozzy stalwart who first hooked up with him in 1986; Mike Inez on bass who had joined Ozzy for the *No More Tears* album; and Kevin Jones on keyboards. To add to the joy of the Ozzy fans, Black Sabbath had been asked to open for him. Ronnie James Dio, who had just returned to the band as lead singer, found the offer offensive and promptly quit, but Sabbath decided to go ahead anyway, and Dio was quickly replaced.

It was, without a doubt, one of Ozzy's most incredible live tours. In his early days in Black Sabbath his fan base was predominantly young teenage males. Now in their forties these fans were still ever-present, but there were just as many in the audience who were in their teens and twenties, and, for the first time ever, the crowds consisted of as many women as they did men. Ozzy, with ironic timing considering he was just about to quit, had finally become cool. The shows were Ozzy at his best. 'Are you fucking crazy? I'm fucking crazy?' he would yell at the crowd every night before hurling buckets of ice-cold water at them – liver and intestines by 1992 were no longer on the menu. During the sing-along song 'Goodbye To Romance' he would bring his three children, now aged nine, eight and seven, on to the stage with him. One would be hoisted on to his shoulders while the others would stand at his side, holding his hand. He may still have been the Prince of Darkness, but Ozzy had a heart and nowadays he wasn't afraid to show it. In October, the tour rolled up in San Antonio, Texas, for Ozzy's first performance in the city since he was arrested ten years earlier. The old Ozzy would no doubt have returned to the scene of the crime, this time to do far worse. But the No More Tours tour was revealing a softer side to his nature and, instead, Ozzy generously donated $10,000 (£6,900) to the caretakers of the Alamo to help with the upkeep of the monument.

On 15 November 1992 in Costa Mesa, California, Ozzy played his last live show. For the second time only since their break-up in 1978, Black Sabbath reunited, with Ozzy joining Tony, 'Geezer' and Bill on stage for four numbers 'Paranoid', 'Iron Man', 'Fairies Wear Boots' and 'Black Sabbath'. As the last strains of 'Black Sabbath' echoed into the night an emotional Ozzy left the stage as a giant neon sign lit up with the message 'Ozzy Osbourne, I'll be back.' The message confirmed what many had suspected all along – that Ozzy might find his vows of retirement exceedingly difficult to keep.

Three days later, Black Sabbath were honored with a star at the Rock Walk on Sunset Boulevard in Hollywood, but after that public appearance, Ozzy disappeared back to Britain to try out a new life as a house-husband. The children were now at an age when they appreciated having their dad around and Ozzy took to his new role immediately, even taking the kids to school. He would spend hours playing with them, but when the children were in their lessons, Ozzy would pace the house, unable to fill his time. He recalls: 'I'd get up, open the fridge, close it, sit down, get up, open it.' To keep himself occupied he began to splash out on expensive treats. Motorbikes, guns and even a pair of night vision goggles in order to see animals running at night. Ozzy bought them all, played with them frantically for a couple of weeks and then dumped them at the back of a cupboard, like a spoilt child bored with the choice of too many toys. Ozzy had genuinely thought he would love retirement, but the reality was that it was driving him crazy. 'I'm one of these people that when I'm on the road I want to be home and then I get back home and do that for a while and end up crawling the walls, itching to get back out there. One thing I discovered is that you have to have something to retire to,' he explained.

Nevertheless, Ozzy grimly persevered. In 1994 he received a Grammy for the Best Metal Performance of the year for 'I Don't Want to Change the World', but otherwise was tempted out of retirement just twice. The first time was to record a version of 'Iron Man' with the Irish band Therapy?, and the second time was for a bizarre duet of 'Born To Be Wild' with Miss Piggy for the *Kermit Unpigged* album. Neither particularly satisfied him, but he had relished the experience of being out of the house for a few days. Ozzy by now was getting on his own nerves as well as Sharon's. A double live album and video of his last tour entitled *Live And Loud* had been a great success, reaching Number Twenty-two in the American charts. It had made him realize just what he was missing. Having vowed never to tour again, he knew he couldn't go back on the road, but he reasoned that there was nothing to stop him from at least writing a few songs. Ozzy teamed up with Steve Vai and, over the course of 1994, between them they came up with forty new songs.

Ozzy enjoyed the process so much that, by the beginning of 1995, he decided that he could stay at home no longer. What was the point of having forty new songs and no one to sing them to? What was the point of retiring, when he still enjoyed work so much? 'What do you do when you get to the top of the mountain and you've stuck your flag in? Go home? "Oh look, that's my fucking great flag?" When the challenge is gone you're dead,' he explained. The next time he retired would be when they lowered him into the ground, he announced. Ozzy was back.

The forty songs he had created with Steve Vai were to form the basis of his 1995 album *Ozzmosis*. In February, Ozzy flew to Paris to begin work. It was a different Ozzy from previous albums. The last album had been made when Ozzy was sober – this time round there were no drugs either. Instead, he would sit around sipping a Diet Coke and nibbling strawberries, and before heading to the studio he would spend two hours working out. To amuse himself he would put on bootleg videos of his old shows that one of the guitarists had brought back from Japan. The concerts were from a few years previously, featuring a bloated Ozzy clearly the worse for drink and drugs. 'I couldn't believe them. I looked like Elvis!' he joked afterwards. But if Ozzy now took more care of his health, in every other way nothing had changed. He was still hyperactive and he still needed to let off steam. Initially, he would amuse himself by decking out the studio with different themes. First it would be a bunker, with a camouflage tent set up in the middle of the studio and Ozzy wearing an army helmet. The next day it would be tropical with palm trees, sun loungers and exotic cocktails and, finally, satanic, with pictures of devils and goats. But Ozzy, as ever, had to step up the tempo. He would take to waiting until the band had eaten before ordering copious amounts of food to be delivered to various individuals at the studio. First of all, twenty large pizzas came addressed to producer Michael

Beinhorn, the next week it was ten three-foot long party-size submarine sandwiches for guitarist Zakk Wylde and, finally, $400 (£275) worth of Chinese food for the engineer. Next came strip-o-grams. To wind up Zakk, Ozzy booked a fifty-five-year-old stripper who weighed 300lbs to turn up to the studios to perform for him. Zakk wasn't amused, but Ozzy was undeterred. If that hadn't make him laugh then perhaps the next day's offering – a male stripper – would . . .

But even these antics weren't enough to keep Ozzy from getting restless and when he unexpectedly disappeared from the studio one day, the rest of the band feared the worst. In the past, Ozzy's disappearances had often lasted for days and involved drink and copious amounts of cocaine. Surely the singer hadn't slipped back into his bad old ways quite so soon? They need not have worried. Ozzy, it emerged, had gone straight to the Virgin Megastore in Paris and come out with two armfuls of CDs and a portable CD player. He'd then headed off to the Left Bank, sat down by the River Seine, eaten some French bread and contentedly listened to music for the rest of the day. But even the cleaned-up Ozzy couldn't help but get into trouble. King Hussein of Jordan had checked in for a short stay at Ozzy's hotel and, when Ozzy arrived back from recording one night, he was stopped by Secret Service agents who thought he looked suspicious. They demanded his ID and questioned him for several minutes, before allowing him up to his room. 'I've been accused of some things in my life, but a terrorist!' Ozzy remarked afterwards.

By the end of 1995 Ozzy was on the road again with his Retirement Sucks tour, leaving no one in any doubt whatsoever about his feelings towards his short-lived departure. A powerful water gun had replaced the buckets of water, and an excited Ozzy would charge up and down the stage laughing manically as he soaked the audience and band alike. With 'Geezer' Butler back on bass, and a lively new band, there was no doubting the fact that Ozzy was glad to get back to touring, but whether his forty-six-year-old body just couldn't cope anymore, or whether it was just sheer bad luck, Ozzy was plagued with health problems. Retirement might have sucked, but working wasn't a bowl of cherries either. In Houston, Ozzy's taxi was involved in a three-car pile up and he ended up with serious whiplash. 'I cannot believe my luck,' he complained afterwards. 'I'm definitely accident prone. If there were 100 people in the street and a flock of birds flew over, the shit would land on me.' Show after show had to be cancelled after Ozzy lost his voice, or suffered from recurring attacks of bronchitis, flu and fatigue. As if that weren't bad enough he suffered a sprained back – the result of another of his infamous frog leaps – and was then diagnosed with arthritis in his hip. 'Well with that, my bad leg and my bad back, I'm a fucking wreck,' Ozzy admitted. 'But no fucker is going to stop me from finishing my tour.'

In desperation, Ozzy resorted to wearing a surgical mask and gloves whenever he appeared in public. He would sit on planes or trains for hours with them on while the band and crew collapsed in hysterical giggles around him, but Ozzy didn't care. By his own admission, he looked like Michael Jackson's ugly brother, but he was determined he wasn't going to get sick again. 'On any normal day for me there could be anywhere from 50-200 people at my meet and greet. Shaking hands and taking pictures with people. And if one of those people has got the shits, or the flu, or bronchitis, or are on their period or pregnant, I'm gonna catch it off them,' he said.

To complicate matters, Ozzy had suffered a severe asthma attack caused by hay fever during a concert in Vancouver. He had tried to give up smoking with the aid of patches earlier in the year and had failed. He was now back up to forty a day and in Vancouver his lungs just gave up. As he began to sing the opening number, he couldn't get his breath and gasped for air. He bravely battled on for two songs, but in the end had to leave the stage for medical treatment, and the show was cancelled. A shaken Ozzy was prescribed Ventolin and told to take two sprays a day, but, terrified of another asthma attack, he began to use it more and more. Eventually, after he used it fifty times before one concert and suffered severe palpitations as a result, Sharon saw red. Ozzy recalls: 'I was so wired that Sharon threw all my inhalants out of the window and threatened to kick my ass if I ever took any more again. I thought my heart was going to come out of my chest. After the show I was up all night.'

In the summer of 1996, Ozzy and the band co-headlined the hugely successful Monsters of Rock festival at Castle Donington alongside Kiss. The show happened to coincide with a time when Sharon was trying to find a new direction for Ozzy, one that built on his reputation, introduced him to a new audience and played to his strengths. Donington, she realized, had done just that; they now needed to come up with a way to capitalize on it. For once, it was Ozzy who came up with the idea, based on a suggestion a friend had made to him ten years earlier. 'He said: "God willing you survive, I could see you in the future having a rock 'n' roll circus – you being the ringmaster,"' Ozzy recalled. But while it was Ozzy's brainwave, it was to be Sharon who would make it work. Naming it Ozzfest, she quickly put together a show featuring some of the best heavy metal talent around – Slayer, Neurosis, Biohazard, Prong, Fear Factory, Danzig – the list went on. And, of course, topping the bill was Ozzy. The festival would have other attractions too – as well as the usual beer, hotdog and merchandising stands, there were stalls offering tattoos and body piercing. 'It's a carnival kind of vibe – a good day out, weather permitting,' Ozzy explained. The first show went ahead on 14 September 1996, followed by two more sell-out dates that year. It was an inspired success, for not only did the festival connect Ozzy firmly with the new generation of rock bands coming through, but it also made a huge amount of money. From Sharon's point of view, it was to be one of her smartest business moves ever, for the festival was to go on to become the most successful tour extravaganza of the 1990s. Ozzy was back once more – not that he'd ever really been away.

The following year Sharon set about putting together Ozzfest 2. The first would be a hard act to follow, but she managed it, reuniting Black Sabbath once more, and ending the festival with a set from Ozzy, 'Geezer' Butler and Tony Iommi. Drummer Bill Ward was not there – different reports put his absence down to either ill-health or a feud with Sharon. Ozzfest played twenty-two shows across America, and Ozzy and Sharon decided it was time to make the States their base. Pop commentator Rick Sky explains: 'Ozzy's not really a musical great, he's an old-fashioned showman and in another lifetime he would have been working in a circus. Sharon realized that his natural home would be America where they liked heavy metal and that vaudeville show. Normally in rock and roll once you're past twenty-five you're a bit too old, but she really regenerated his career.'

Ozzy and Sharon sold their luxury mansion in Chalfont St Peter, Buckinghamshire – a house formerly owned by Dirk Bogarde – bought a new place in the nearby village of Jordans, which would be their holiday home, and bought a bigger place in Los Angeles. Ozzy was sad to go. For all his flamboyance in many ways he was a typical Englishman who liked nothing better than relaxing over a pint at the pub. In the 1980s he had invested in a wine bar in Stafford and for many years he would say his favorite night out was a drink at his local, the Red Lion at Sutton near Newport Salop in Staffordshire. 'With all the exotic places I go to in the world I find this is a place I can relax and unwind and people take me as being me. I'm not Ozzy Osbourne on stage when I'm here, I'm Ozzy at home, this is like my second home,' he once explained.

In November, Ozzy released *The Ozzman Cometh* a greatest hits package featuring some old Sabbath songs, some of his best-known solo work and a new song 'Back On Earth'. But the partial reunion at Ozzfest had given Ozzy, Tony and 'Geezer' a taste of the old days, a taste of the early magic that had created heavy rock way back in the early 1970s. And they wanted more. Bill Ward was contacted, rehearsals secretly organized and on the 4 and 5 December 1997 at the National Exhibition Centre in Birmingham, England – fittingly the place where it had all started – Black Sabbath were reunited. Back on stage for a whole show for the first time in nineteen years the band went down a storm. Such a storm in fact, that it was quickly announced that Sabbath would headline the following year's UK Ozzfest at the Milton Keynes Bowl on 20 June 1998. Sadly, it would not go according to plan, with Bill Ward's decades of ill-health catching up with him. Like Ozzy, Bill was a heavy drinker and drug-user both during and after the Sabbath years and he suffered a mild heart attack in rehearsals. It was enough to prevent him playing but to the crowd's delight, it was not enough to prevent him taking a bow at the end of the show with the rest of the band. Delighted to have his old friend back on stage with him, Ozzy showed his appreciation in his own inimitable way – pulling down his pants and mooning in front of 60,000 ecstatic fans. As he explained later: 'I never pre-planned 99.9 per cent of the things I've done. I've dressed in women's clothes, I've dressed as a Nazi. I've gone on stage naked. I've gone on so drunk I didn't even know I did a show. I've done so many stupid things, but it's all part of Ozzy.'

Later that year Ozzfest 3 toured the States, with Ozzy headlining alongside bands such as Motörhead, Megadeth, Tool, Limp Bizkit and Incubus. But Black Sabbath was by now becoming as big a pull as solo Ozzy. In September, they released *Reunion,* a live album recorded at the previous year's Birmingham shows, and also including two new studio tracks, the first time Ozzy, 'Geezer', Tony and Bill had recorded together in twenty years. It was followed by the announcement that Sabbath were going back on the road again with a full-scale Reunion tour, kicking off in Phoenix, Arizona on New Year's Eve. The tour continued until February 1999, but was not without problems. No sooner had they started before two shows in Salt Lake City, Utah and Denver, Colorado were postponed due to illness. Flu was the official reason, but sensing impending disaster, the band approached Vinnie Appice to be on permanent stand-by should anything befall drummer Bill Ward. So convinced were they that this would happen that they even set up Appice's drum kit at the back of the stage behind Bill's, so that he would be able to go on at a moment's notice. In the event it was Ozzy, not Bill, who fell ill. Ozzy's body had struggled to cope with the strains of touring for some years. He may have been in a lot better physical shape but by 1998 Ozzy had hit fifty, and in the middle of the tour he developed serious throat problems. He had suffered from them on and off for years, but when he developed a throat nodule – an irritating growth on his larynx – several shows had to be put on hold.

Still, performing live again had become such a buzz for Sabbath that they weren't going to give up now and, after a brief rest, they hit the road again for their Last

Supper tour – the highlight of Ozzfest 1999. By December 1999 they had played just about every country on the map. None of them had been happy with the messy way the band had fallen apart in 1978. Twenty-one years later, it was time to bow out again – this time in style. On 21 and 22 December, the band returned to Birmingham to play two final sell-out shows. They announced that this would be the last time that the original Black Sabbath would ever play together.

It was the end of an era. Not that it worried Ozzy in the slightest. By now the singer had far bigger fish to fry. Not only was he almost permanently in demand as a solo singer, in amongst the touring he'd teamed up with Busta Rhymes to record a rap version of 'Iron Man' and had also provided a song for the *South Park* soundtrack. He was also the ringmaster and proud architect of Ozzfest, by now the biggest rock festival on the circuit. If, in the early 1980s, Ozzy had been in danger of becoming a bloated pantomime shadow of his former self, those days were well and truly past. Ozzy had re-invented himself and Ozzfest was now a must-play date for anybody who was anyone in the rock world. Today, it is still as successful as ever, grossing $20 million (£14 million) every summer, and shows no sign of abating. To Ozzy's huge relief and pleasure, the 1990s hadn't made him respectable, but they had certainly made him rich.

chapter ten

The Osbournes

6 *I know I'm just some bloke who won the Lottery,
it could easily have gone the other way for me.* 9

THE OLD MILLENNIUM had ended on a high for Ozzy, but the new one started with a crushing blow – the death of his mother Lillian. Although life on the road meant he had seen little of her for many years, they had remained close. 'My mother could phone me up now, and I'd give her my life, she gave me a life,' he once explained. In the end there was nothing he could do to help her. Her death came peacefully in her sleep on 10 April, 2001. She was eighty-five but Ozzy was still heart-broken. Although she suffered from diabetes and kidney problems, he had been to see her a week earlier and she had seemed fine. If Ozzy had been devastated by the death of his father twenty-three years earlier, it was nothing compared to how he felt about losing his mother. Terrified that he might go to pieces completely he decided not to attend the funeral. 'They fuck me up too much,' he explained. 'It might have pushed me over the edge. I thought I was going nuts. I was driving around with spears. I was near the dark side. It was like waking up with the world's worst hangover, but I hadn't had a drink. I'm glued together with medication. I'm on everything – proper psychotic medication. If I don't pop pills I lose it. I'm a fucking nutter.'

By now Ozzy's ill health was a serious and permanent problem. He had consulted the best doctors that money could buy in both Britain and America, but all had come to the same sad conclusion, that Ozzy's heavy use of drink and drugs over the decades had taken its toll. During his days on the road he would notoriously try anything and everything to get a new and different high; he had even stayed awake for two entire weeks, simply to see the effects of sleep deprivation on his brain. (Today, ironically, he suffers from insomnia.) Doctors told him that the years of abuse had caused a chemical imbalance in his brain, which needed to be controlled with prescription drugs. In addition, there was Ozzy's genetic predisposition towards mental illness. Nowadays he sees a psychiatrist almost daily, and an addiction therapist has put him on Prozac and 200mg of Zoloft to help control his insecurity and depression. He has not touched illegal drugs for twelve years, believing the experience could end up killing him. 'I'm on psychiatric and psychotic medication. I'm on antidepressants,' he explained. 'If I was to add ecstasy to my prescription drugs, I'd explode. There'd be a pair of shoes on the floor and a splat on the ceiling!'

The years have also taken their toll physically. These days Ozzy moves slowly, and has a stoop and a shuffling gait including a slight limp. His hearing is poor and his hands shake and, at times, he seems to struggle to get his words out. The exact cause of his problems remains a mystery; rumors abound in the music business that he has suffered a stroke or has Parkinson's Disease, but Ozzy insists that is not the case. 'For a while I thought I'd got Parkinson's, but my sister Jean told me it was just a hereditary tremor,' he says. When performing he is no longer capable of the famous frog jumps, nor can he easily run backwards and forwards from one end of the stage to the other. His voice can no longer reach the high notes and his set is chosen accordingly, leaving out songs that he can no longer manage. As a young man in Black Sabbath, he once predicted that he would not make forty, and Britain's hit music station Radio One prepared his obituary back in 1978. Today Ozzy has adjusted his sights, but still says: 'I know I ain't going to fucking live to be an old man. I know that. My psychiatrist can't understand how I'm still walking and talking. I should have been long gone.'

It may now be over a decade since Ozzy touched illegal drugs, but even with the help of his therapists and doctors, he still finds it hard to keep himself on the straight and narrow. The addictive personality that emerged in his teens is still present in middle age, and when asked recently what he would now consider his addictions, he answered 'Everything.' On the Howard Stern show in the States in early 2002, he revealed that he was addicted to Viagra, taking up to fifteen pills a day. He had started using them to boost his flagging sex life after being unable to make love for a month, but said he enjoyed the taste so much that he couldn't stop chewing them. Over the years he has tried and failed on countless occasions to give up smoking – he finally gave up cigarettes for good in the summer of 2001 after getting together with his old friends from Black Sabbath and discovering he was the only one who still smoked, but today he still uses nicotine chewing gum to help cope with the cravings, and enjoys the occasional cigar. Although he successfully stayed off alcohol for almost five years in the 1990s, he would eat up to ten Snickers chocolate bars a day as compensation. These days he drinks intermittently, but is terrified by the thought of being without access to it. So worried was he by the possibility of liquor stores and supermarkets being closed down by the millennium bug that he buried stashes of vodka in the garden of his home in Buckinghamshire. To enable him to carry out his covert operation while Sharon was asleep he installed huge floodlights, which the neighbors immediately complained about. The story made the local papers when Ozzy insisted that the reason for the lights was that he found it difficult to sleep and liked to unwind with a little late-night gardening. Ozzy recalls: 'On the millennium I kept nipping out for a drink. After a while Sharon said, "Oi, you're

drunk and where's all this effing vodka coming from?"'
By his own admission, he could write 'The Guide to
Rehab Clinics' – he has stayed at more than fourteen
since the early 1980s – but says he finds the sober life
boring. He would dearly love to be able to drink in
moderation, and will go for days sipping only diet soda
and mineral water, but then suddenly he will crack and
drink the house dry. He explained recently: 'Sometimes
I have one and then suddenly the fridge is empty and
I'm throwing bottles through the window. I'm a frustrated alcoholic. The dream of me having a social drink
is bollocks.'

Yet despite his growing health problems, the past
three years have seen Ozzy in just as much demand
musically as ever. Despite the vow that Black Sabbath
was no more, the new decade started in much the same
way as the last one ended – with another Black Sabbath
tour. Just six months into 2000 Ozzy played a show in
Los Angeles for KROQ radio and surprised everyone by
reuniting with the group. The following year, Black
Sabbath was back once more at Ozzfest 2001 playing
alongside Slipknot, Papa Roach, Marilyn Manson,
Linkin Park and Black Label Society.

But if Ozzy thought he was proving popular in 2001,
he had no idea what was around the corner, and
October of that year was to prove a landmark in the
singer's life. Not only did he release *Down To Earth*, his
first solo album for six years and a Number Four success
in the American album charts, but, to his delight, Play
Station 2 created an Ozzy video game entitled *Ozzy
Osbourne's Black Skies* – a 3D combat game set within
worlds inspired by his music. More significantly, however, October was the month that MTV moved in.

A TV show based on Ozzy had been considered for
quite some time. In his previous LA home Ozzy lived
next door to legendary 1950s crooner Pat Boone, and
the couple had struck up an unlikely friendship.

Scriptwriters, intrigued by this relationship, spent time with the Osbournes in order to come up with a sitcom based on Ozzy's life, but soon realized that the Osbourne family's humor was far funnier than anything they could write. Instead, they suggested a fly-on-the-wall documentary series charting everyday life chez the Osbournes. Sharon agreed a fee of $290,000 (£200,000) and a full-time TV crew moved in, setting up twelve cameras and staying with the family for five months, twenty-four hours a day. The only rules were that the bedroom and bathroom were out of bounds, and that Ozzy's eldest daughter Aimee, then eighteen, would not be involved. Aimee, by far the most normal member of the family, had for some time felt the odd-one-out. As well as designing her own jewelry, she had followed her father into the music business as a singer, but her taste in music was much gentler – Enya rather than nu-metal – and for the duration of the series she said she would prefer to live in a nearby flat. Ozzy's droll sixteen-year-old son Jack would stay, as would his pink-haired, punk rock daughter Kelly, aged seventeen.

Ozzy was slightly bemused, but went along with Sharon's idea. Besides, at the time, he had other things on his mind – his first solo tour for seven years. Not that financially he needed to tour again. The year had started with Sharon and Ozzy debuting on the British Rich List with a joint fortune of $58 million (£40 million), more than half of it generated by Sharon through her management company and Ozzfest. Ozzy had sold more than 170 million records in his career, and had earned and lost a fortune several times. But, with Sharon at his side, bad management and uncontrolled spending were in the past. Finally, in his fifties, Ozzy was a very wealthy man. The money, however, would not stop him doing what he loved most. 'Until there comes a day when the band stop having fun, until the kids stop having fun, until I stop having fun, I'll probably keep going,' he explained.

Just a few weeks in to the tour, however, the ever-accident prone Ozzy fell stepping out of the shower and hurt his leg. Unaware that he had actually fractured a bone, he continued to perform for another week before the pain became unbearable. Doctors prescribed the powerful painkiller Vicodin, and immediately ordered Ozzy to rest his leg and stop touring, to prevent further injury. Ozzy, however, had never paid much attention to what doctors had told him in the past and he wasn't going to start now. He did take Vicodin, though predictably not in the prescribed amounts. 'When people tell me take one every five hours, I'll take five every one hour,' he admitted. Rather than resting his leg, he continued to chase his recalcitrant pets around the garden. Three weeks later, he was back on the road again and on 23 December played an emotional World Trade Center benefit show at the Meadowlands Stadium in New Jersey. Ozzy also visited Ground Zero and was presented by New York firefighters and police with an iron cross made from steel from the wreckage of the World Trade Center. The cross meant a lot to him as America was now his adopted home. He had been in New York at the time of the 11 September tragedy and had been deeply moved by what had happened, even changing the tour name from Black Christmas to Merry Mayhem as a mark of respect to the families who lost loved ones. In addition, proceeds from merchandise sold at a special Ozz Bless America booth at every show would go direct to the fund set up for firefighters and their families.

In February 2002 Ozzy's tour rolled on, taking in Japan, Korea, Canada, Germany and a first-ever stop in Alaska. But if the frozen North was going crazy for the Prince of Darkness, it was nothing compared to what was happening elsewhere in the States. On 5 March, the first episode of *The Osbournes* premiered on MTV. The show was an instant hit, its early cult following quickly turning into mass-market appeal, with more than six million viewers every week – the highest rated show in the channel's twenty-year history. The fly-on-the-wall series was a revelation – a real-life cross between *The Simpsons, The Beverly Hillbillies* and *The Addams Family* – showing the Prince of Darkness as he'd never been seen before. Not surprisingly, the whole of America – mums, dads and their kids – lapped it up. In the show Ozzy pads around the house in make-up, wearing black track-suit bottoms and a black t-shirt, his long hair tied back and his arms covered in tattoos. Almost every other word he utters is a swearword, but otherwise the wildest man in rock appears every inch the archetypal sit-com old-codger dad – fifty-three years of age, genial, flustered and completely baffled by his family and the modern world. Just ten years ago his albums had been slapped with parental warning stickers, now men's magazines were approaching him for parenting advice. A baffled Ozzy says: 'I've become everybody's American father and I'm not even American.'

The show is funny primarily because Ozzy isn't actually trying to be. We see him struggling to change a bin liner and collecting his incontinent dog from the vet. One of the most hilarious episodes is one in which he battles unsuccessfully for several minutes with the TV remote control. He can get no further than the Weather Channel and somehow seems to set off a mobile phone in another room, and then the shower upstairs. In desperation he yells for Jack to come and help him and, after patiently teaching his dad how the device works, Ozzy and Jack sit down arm-in-arm to watch a History Channel documentary.

It is that unbeatable combination of eccentricity, celebrity and lack of self-awareness that makes the show compulsive viewing. As MTV Entertainment President

Brian Graden explains: 'It's the juxtaposition of the fantastical rock-star life with the ordinary and the everyday. In one episode we start where he's just trying to turn on the vacuum cleaner. Before anything gets off the ground, you're thinking, "Am I really seeing Ozzy Osbourne trying to turn on the vacuum cleaner?"' Or, as Ozzy puts it: 'I suppose Americans get a kick out of watching a crazy Brit family like us make complete fools out of ourselves every week.'

Undoubtedly at the heart of the show's appeal is Ozzy's relationship with his wayward children, Jack and Kelly. When they were younger Ozzy would tease them by feeding their pet parrot by placing food on his tongue. The bird was forced to put its head in Ozzy's mouth and the kids were terrified that one day Ozzy would snap its head off. Today, however, it's the kids who are in charge, frequently breaking their 2am curfews, smoking, drinking and getting tattoos. What is particularly funny is watching Ozzy – who had done all these things and worse by the time he was their age – struggle to establish family values. He may have the big house in Beverly Hills, he may still be a little wild, but at home he is everyday dad – beset with the same problems as parents the world over. As Kelly and Jack are preparing for a night out, Ozzy calls them into the kitchen for a little fatherly advice before they go. 'Don't get drunk or stoned tonight,' he says. 'I'll be fucking pissed off because I can't! And if you're gonna have sex, wear a condom.' It might not be the way most dads would phrase it, but the sentiment is still the same. In other episodes the roles are reversed, with the kids chiding Ozzy, on one occasion telling him off for lighting a cigar. 'Fucking $3 million house and I have to stand outside and smoke,' Ozzy complains. When Kelly accuses Ozzy of never hearing anything she says, he ripostes: 'You've not been standing in front of thirty million decibels for thirty-five years. Just write me a note.'

To viewers' amazement, the man who bit the heads off a bat and a dove is actually never happier than when he's simply watching TV or messing about at home. However, with Jack and Kelly around there is little chance of peace, and as yet another fight breaks out between the two warring teenagers, he yells: 'I love you all. I love you more than my life. But you're all fucking mad!' In some ways they are clearly their father's children. They swear, they look strange and they've inherited his passion for heavy metal. At Kelly's seventeenth birthday party, Ozzy tells her friends not to smoke and to turn down the deafening music. Ironically, the man who played it louder than anyone else is forced to leave the room, complaining: 'It's music to get a brain seizure by.' As a result of her exposure on the TV show, Kelly was invited to join forces with Incubus to record a heavy-metal cover of Madonna's pop hit 'Papa Don't Preach', which featured on *The Osbourne Family Album*, a CD of old and new songs hand-picked by members of the family. Jack, who works as a part-time talent scout for Epic Records, produced the track. Kelly says: 'I didn't choose the song. My mom did. I'm kind of crapping myself because I don't think I'm a very good singer.'

Jack, meanwhile, refuses to go to school on time, orders pizza at midnight, invites his friends to play pool in the middle of the night, hangs out with strippers and has been caught smoking a joint. In one episode of the show, Ozzy is seen disarming Jack, who was planning to go for a night on the town carrying a knife. Ozzy searches for a hiding place for the weapon, in the end settling for a spot where Jack will never look, underneath a banana in the fruit basket. In another, we see the family nanny, Melinda, picking up Jack from school camp, where he confesses he did nothing but sit and throw rocks at the teachers all day. And when his new bulldog Lola makes a mess in the living room, he blames his mother. 'You know why my dog's dysfunctional? Because he's angry at you – just like me,' he says. In some ways, though, Ozzy's children appear much wiser, perhaps having learnt from their dad's mistakes. On one occasion Kelly returns home from a nightclub telling her dad that she had left early because everyone was taking cocaine. Ozzy admitted afterwards: 'I was really proud of her. It don't sound like one of my kids. If it was me I'd still be down that club sniffing the ashtrays.' Jack simply finds his parents embarrassing. His dad walks around the whole time in his underwear, he complains, while his mum flashes at his friends and asks if they think she's sexy.

What emerges in the show is that Sharon, who in 2002 was listed among the world's most beautiful women by *People* magazine in America, clearly rules the roost. She obviously adores Ozzy – to the kids' horror they are openly affectionate with each other around the house – and she would do anything to protect him. At a restaurant in Beverly Hills last year, she went crazy when Ozzy returned from the men's toilets and told her that a man had approached him and offered him cocaine. Ozzy, who hadn't touched the drug for over a decade, was horrified, but his reaction was nothing compared to Sharon's. Jumping out of her seat, she ran to get the manager, pointed the man out and demanded that the manager call the police. It was too much for Ozzy to handle and he hurried out of the restaurant: 'And all I can hear is this huge fucking row going off behind me,' he recalls. "You motherfucker drug addict offering my husband drugs, I want the police here, the manager. . ."' But while Sharon clearly wears the trousers, there are limits and there is a hilarious exchange in one episode when she suggests that they fill the stage with bubbles at the next concert. 'Bubbles!' shouts a horrified Ozzy, 'Sharon, I'm the Prince of fucking Darkness!'

Although they spend most episodes feuding amongst themselves, the Osbournes unite spectacularly in a furious dispute with their neighbors over the never-ending racket that goes on in the middle of the night. A racket, ironically, that the *neighbors* are making. In what must surely be total anathema to a heavy rocker, the neighbors invite friends round for folk-singing sessions, bashing out tunes such as 'Kumbayah' and 'He's Got The Whole World In His Hands'. 'You wankers have no respect for your neighbors!' yells Ozzy, as the rest of the family toss French bread, bagels, cheese and a large ham over the fence. The ham is the final straw, and the next day Sharon is visited by the police. Far from being repentant, she is so incensed by one of the neighbors in particular that she seethes: 'I want to hold him down and piss on his head!' 'That's going a bit far, mum,' scolds Kelly, demonstrating rare restraint.

Ozzy's house proves almost as fascinating as the family that lives in it. The mansion, which sits in the streets above Sunset Boulevard, bears a sign on the gate: 'Never mind the dog, beware of the owner', and the arched front doors have crucifix spy holes, above which sits a large demonic gargoyle. Inside it is a fascinating mix of the macabre and the mundane. In the opening episode, the family are seen moving in, their packing boxes labeled 'pots and pans', 'linen', 'devil heads' and 'dead things'. There are crucifixes on the walls, alongside paintings of Sodom and Gomorrah and angels and devils, but in the kitchen are comfortable cream sofas and chintz curtains, and there is a formal dining room with velvet chairs, drapes, and an ornate chandelier. Not surprisingly, it is the least-used room in the house. Apart from at Christmas and at Thanksgiving, the family never sits down to meals together.

Ozzy has his own sitting room decorated in burnished wood and velvet, with leather chairs and a gothic tone. It houses a giant screen television, a drawing table where he likes to unwind by painting, and a bathroom with a framed bat on the wall and a urinal. Says Kelly:

'We had a urinal put in here because Dad always pees on the toilet seat.' On the bookshelves, amidst biographies of The Beatles and books about aviation and World War Two, are several crucifixes and a grinning skull. On one shelf sits a framed letter from Kelly, written for Ozzy on his fiftieth birthday, when she was fourteen. It reads: 'Dear Daddy, Happy 50th birthday. I hope you have a really good day. Your party will be the event of the year. I can't tell you how proud I am of you. I love you so much. I hope you like your present. I spent a lot. It's one of a kind. I love you, Kelly.'

Sharon has her own sitting room, too, and there is a games room used mainly by the children and their friends, containing pinball machines and a billiards table. Upstairs are the bedrooms and Ozzy's gym. Kelly has two rooms, decorated in pink and white, and two bathrooms, while Jack's room is the archetypal teenage bachelor pad, with a huge TV, VCR and DVD, an extensive record collection and a studded leather bed decorated with a Celtic cross. In the perfectly manicured back garden, there is a beautifully landscaped pool complete with rocks, a waterfall, and a waterslide. There is also a secret grotto, a Jacuzzi and lots of statues.

Like any typical sitcom house, The Osbournes' home is full of animals. The family own three cats and seven dogs – Chihuahuas Lulu and Martin, Japanese chins Maggie and New Baby, Jack's bulldog Lola, a white Pomeranian called Minnie and black Pomeranian Pipi, belonging to Aimee. When Pipi went missing for two months early in 2002, Ozzy was heartbroken and joined forces with an American TV station to offer $1,000 (£690) reward for her safe return. The man who was once considered a threat to all living creatures is frequently seen cooing and kissing the dogs, yet at the same time the animals provide a regular source of frustration. 'Some days you're fucking pissed off – you stub your foot on the fucking bedpost or you find the cat's crapped on the carpet. Mind you, in my house, cat crap and dog crap are a fucking given, with 9,000 fucking creatures crapping all over the place,' he complains. 'A rock star is supposed to say, "Get me the Vicodins", or "Run me a bath with fucking Perrier water". I get fucking dog shit up to the elbows and an earful of fucking abuse.'

The series was entered for an Emmy award (which it won) and on 26 May 2002 transferred to satellite television in Britain where it received similar rave reviews. Over 500,000 viewers tuned in to watch the opening episode, beating ITV1 in homes that had digital, cable or satellite TV. As Sharon says shrewdly: 'I knew it would be big. Ozzy is not the kind of guy who comes home carrying his briefcase at the end of a hard day's work.'

To add to the accolades in 2002, Ozzy also received his own star on Hollywood's prestigious Walk Of Fame and then to his own amazement – let alone to the astonishment of the establishment – was invited to meet the President at the White House. 'I thought I'd be on a Wanted poster on his wall, not invited to his place for tea,' was his reaction on hearing the news. The occasion was the prestigious annual White House Press Correspondents' Dinner. Ozzy was honored, but, never being a great respecter of pomp and ceremony, arrived with an MTV crew in tow, along with several burly security guards who screamed at guests, including senators and congressmen, to 'move the fuck out of the way.' At the start of his speech, President Bush introduced his guests: 'Washington power brokers, celebrities, Hollywood stars, Ozzy Osbourne . . . okay, Ozzy might have been a mistake.' The audience erupted in laughter and cheers and a delighted Ozzy jumped on a chair to wave. White House security staff had carefully placed him on Table 168, well away from the top table at which the President was seated, but as the evening wore on, Ozzy spotted his chance and carefully crept forward. When he was just ten feet away, the President noticed him.

Ozzy put his hands together as if saying a prayer and pointed them towards Bush as a mark of respect. The President nodded in acknowledgement, while Bush's advisors, seated at his side, nervously held their breath. So far, so good. But Ozzy just couldn't pass up an opportunity like this. Grabbing a fistful of his long black hair, now dyed red at the ends, he took another step forward and yelled, 'You should wear your hair like mine!' Bush blushed momentarily and didn't reply, but, significantly, he didn't move either. Anyone else taking such a liberty with the President of the United States would have been swiftly ushered away after a quick nod towards security, and there'd have been an immediate inquiry into how it could have happened in the first place. But hell, this was Ozzy Osbourne! America's favo crazy guy, dad and bad boy, Dubya's hero. Bush's face broke into a grin as he leaned forward and shouted back: 'Second term, Ozzy!'

But Ozzy wasn't just in demand with the President of the United States. Only weeks later, he was invited to perform 'Paranoid' for the Queen at her Golden Jubilee Pop Concert at Buckingham Palace in London on 3 June 2002. The guest artists included some of the pop world's greatest stars, including Sir Paul McCartney, Elton John, Eric Clapton, Rod Stewart and Tom Jones. A Royal spokesman, aware of Ozzy's reputation concerning small creatures, joked: 'I think I can guarantee he will be kept away from the corgis. Ozzy may not be one of the Queen's favorites, but she wanted a concert to reflect Britain's music heritage.' Ozzy's flamboyant past, his bad language and his demonic appearance ensure that he will always have his detractors, and the royal invitation predictably went down badly in some quarters, with the *Daily Express* newspaper running a page-long feature on the subject, under the headline: 'He glorified drugs, drink and Satan, so why has Ozzy Osbourne been asked to play for the Queen?'

Ozzy was inclined to agree with such sentiments, and the decision to invite him to appear at the Palace was one that astonished him as much as it delighted him. It was also one that made him incredibly nervous, particularly as rehearsals for the show had got off to such a blistering start. The day before the concert Ozzy had just finished rehearsing his song when fire broke out inside Buckingham Palace. Twenty fire engines rushed to the scene as smoke billowed out of the roof, and the rehearsals were hastily cancelled, as hundreds of people were led from the burning building. It was the first time the Palace had been evacuated since World War Two. It was nothing to do with Ozzy, but naturally it was just Ozzy's luck to be there when it happened.

After a scare like that Ozzy was taking no chances and, minutes before he was due to appear on stage, he was found by concerned band members kneeling in the wings, praying. His prayers to God were not to ask that he give a good performance on such a prestigious occasion, nor even for an appreciative audience who would shout and scream for more. Instead, Ozzy was praying that he would remember not to swear in front of such exalted company. 'I'm on my best behavior. I don't want to spend the rest of my life in the Tower,' he explained. 'I read about all these rules for the performers about not going near the wildlife or worrying the ducks. I mustn't drop my trousers, no bad language, or perhaps a trap door will open.'

When his moment came, it was a classic Ozzy performance. He stumbled on stage, chewing gum and yelling into his microphone before comedian Lenny Henry had even finished announcing his arrival. Within seconds he had the Union flag-waving crowd on their feet, chanting his name as he charged up and down the stage, belting out 'Paranoid' for all he was worth. When the song ended the patriotic singer gave a slight bow to the Royal Box and yelled 'God Save the Queen', while

Princes William and Harry laughed and cheered and applauded furiously, with their hands above their heads.

After the concert, the celebrities lined up as the Queen took to the stage to meet them. Standing next to Rod Stewart, Ozzy couldn't believe it when the Queen stopped right in front of him and thanked him for appearing. 'She said, "I understand you're quite the wild one." I just went, "Heh, heh, heh",' recalls Ozzy, who kept his left hand in his pocket throughout the encounter, fearing the Queen might faint if she saw the O-z-z-y tattoo on his fingers. Ozzy smiled politely and remembered not to swear, but as Sharon explained afterwards, the brief meeting predictably still went less than smoothly. 'He didn't know what to call her and he was all flustered and he ended up calling her "your worship", she revealed. 'It was like something out of a *Monty Python* sketch.' To make matters worse, popular puppet Kermit the Frog – a fellow performer at the show – had been sitting on Rod Stewart's shoulder. Sharon recalls: 'Rod said "Get that flaming frog off my shoulder" and he punched the frog and the frog went "blip" right on to Ozzy's shoulder as the Queen comes down the line. It could only happen to my husband that he meets the Queen of England, he calls her your worship, and he's got a flaming frog on his shoulder.'

At the after-show party, however, it was Sharon who let her hair down, more than making up for her husband's careful behavior. The Queen opted for an early night, but all the other members of the Royal Family were there and all of them asked to meet Ozzy. To liven things up, Sharon cheekily pinched the bottoms of Prince Charles and William and Harry and also squeezed the breasts of Prince Charles' partner Camilla Parker Bowles, telling her: 'You've got gorgeous tits.' Sharon laughed afterwards: 'Everybody was so straight-laced. But I swore in front of them and I'm like "Come on, let's have a party." Camilla just stood there and let me grab her tits. The princes were shocked that this mad old rocker woman was pinching their asses. Charles just sort of raised his eyebrow.' Ozzy, however, was less laid-back about his wife's performance. 'My eyeballs nearly flew out of my head,' he said afterwards. Meanwhile, Prince William sought out Ozzy to tell him that he should have played more Black Sabbath songs during his set. Says Ozzy: 'I told him if I had done Black Sabbath, the fucking Royal Box would have turned to stone, and the Archbishop of Canterbury would have had to douse them in holy water.'

On the music front, Ozzy had a new single out called 'Dreamer', which made Number Eighteen on the British charts. He planned to spend the rest of the summer as usual on tour with Ozzfest 2002, performing alongside singers half his age. Middle age, he insists, has never suited him. 'If I only ever hung out with people my own age, all we'd sit and talk about is mortgages and hysterectomies! Young people have young thoughts and it's a real tonic,' he says. In July Ozzy and Sharon planned to celebrate their twentieth wedding anniversary by re-marrying. 'Other people,' Ozzy couldn't help but quip, when asked about their plans on a British TV chat show. Meanwhile, a second series of the hugely popular *The Osbournes* was due to start filming shortly afterwards.

All in all, it was going to be a great summer and there was a huge amount for the whole family to look forward to. After the ups and downs of his incredible career, Ozzy had finally been dealt a decent hand. The Buckingham Palace concert over, the Osbourne clan flew back to America on a huge high. Life, for once, seemed as near perfect as possible.

Even Ozzy, by now well used to life's cruel habit of kicking him in the teeth as soon as things began to look up for him, could never for one second have anticipated the tragedy that lay ahead.

chapter eleven

Heaven and Hell

*6 This year I've been from the gates of Buckingham Palace
to the gates of hell. 9*

OZZY has always been something of a hypochondriac. He is always convinced that the slightest cough and sniffle are actually life-threatening diseases and, as a result, has spent years visiting a whole array of doctors about his various ailments – real or imagined. Arriving back in Los Angeles from his Royal performance in Britain he decided, after the exertions of his trip, to check himself in to a local hospital for a full physical examination, where doctors found several polyps on his colon. They weren't serious, but Ozzy was so shocked that he could have developed the growths without even knowing about them that he started to nag Sharon into getting herself a medical too. 'He bothered me night and day, so I finally gave in and went. I absolutely hate doctors, and hospitals even more. But to make him happy I went along for the check-up,' she recalls.

Initial blood tests showed she was anemic. Suspecting internal bleeding, doctors decided to investigate further and on 3 July Sharon underwent a colonoscopy, where a flexible lighted tube is used to examine the lower intestine for any abnormal growths. Thinking nothing more of it, she flew to New York the following day to be with her children. Son Jack was doing a round of media interviews, normally shy Aimee was being photographed for a New York magazine and Kelly had just begun recording her first album. After a successful first day in the recording studio, they returned to Kelly's apartment where Sharon picked up an urgent message on the answer machine asking her to contact the hospital immediately. She called and, to her shock, was told the devastating news that the tests had uncovered cancerous growths and that she must return immediately for surgery. Ozzy, who was back in Los Angeles rehearsing for the annual summer Ozzfest was simply not prepared for the diagnosis. 'When I heard the news I simply and utterly fell apart at the seams,' he recalls. 'This is the love of my life and the thought that I could lose her was more than I could bear.'

Sharon and the children flew back in tears to Los Angeles the next day. Ozzy met them at the airport with one of their pet dogs in an attempt to cheer them all up, but by the evening the Osbournes' doctor had received a phone call asking him to attend the family home urgently. When he arrived, he discovered to his surprise that he had not in fact been called out to treat Sharon, who was remaining remarkably strong despite her worst fears. Instead he was needed to sedate Ozzy, who, confronted with the thought of losing his wife, had just not been able to hold it together any longer. 'He was hysterical, a complete wreck, just terrified,' says Sharon. 'I started feeling worse for him and my children than I did for myself.'

The two of them stayed awake all night, holding each other, until Sharon's appointment for surgery at noon the next day at Los Angeles' Cedars-Sinai Medical Center. After the four-hour operation, Sharon needed a blood transfusion of three pints, but the worst was yet to come. Two lymph nodes removed during the operation had tested positive for cancerous cells, which meant that the disease had spread outside the colon. To fight it, Sharon needed to start an immediate three-month course of chemotherapy.

Ozzy, determined to be there for his wife, announced he would be taking a three-week break from his headlining duties on Ozzfest to be by Sharon's side when she began the chemotherapy on 29 July. 'This has been one

At Home With Ozzy – *The Osbournes* has earned him the praise of President Bush for his parenting skills

© David Mansell / Camera Press London

With the very recently
arrived Jack, born on
8 November 1985
mirrorpix.com

Above: The Osbournes *en famille* – *I Love Lucy* meets *The Simpsons* by way of *The Addams Family*
mirrorpix.com

Right: Ozzy with Sharon, his second wife and manager. Her father, Don Arden, charged her $1.5 million to buy out Ozzy's contract
mirrorpix.com

Top: Ozzy and Sharon in 1987. Her management of his career has helped to take Ozzy to the top
mirrorpix.com

Below: With Aimee *(left)*, Jack and Kelly *(right)* in the late 1980s *mirrorpix.com*

of the hardest decisions I've had to make and I'm hoping that my fans will understand, but I'm burning up inside. I'm falling apart more than she is. It's like someone has taken my heart away. I have to go home,' he explained. Ozzy's heart was certainly in the right place, but after just one chemotherapy session, Sharon decided it would be better if from now on she went to the hospital alone. On the very first visit to the hospital Ozzy had passed out, and in the end the doctors had spent more time looking after him than her!

Not for the first time since they'd met it was Sharon who was holding the whole thing together, with her own irrepressible sense of humor. 'Why'd they have to find it in my bum of all places?' she asked. 'It's embarrassing. I mean, why couldn't I have had a cute heart-shaped polyp on my vagina?' she joked. Meanwhile, as an act of solidarity and love for Sharon, Ozzy announced that should she lose her hair during the treatment he would shave his head. 'We'll be the Baldbournes together,' he joked. But behind the smiles Ozzy was not coping at all well. Most of his days were now spent pacing up and down at home, in tears, simply unable to comprehend the thought of a future without Sharon. As he explained: 'People say to me, "Ozzy, you've got to be strong for Sharon." And I'm not Superman, you know. Shares in Kleenex must have gone up tenfold.' Sharon understood Ozzy's fear, but she couldn't bear to see him falling apart in front of her eyes. Ozzy had never been very good at coping with enforced absences from work. He loved his family and home, but inevitably went stir-crazy if he found himself cooped up at home with nothing to do. Added to that, his grief and worry made it impossible for Sharon and the children to cheer him up. In the end Sharon decided on the only course of action she knew would help. It was the one thing that had helped Ozzy at the bleakest times of his life. When drink and drugs addictions threatened to destroy him, when friends died, when financial crisis loomed, the only thing that could get Ozzy out of bed and back on track was his beloved music. A week later – on Sharon's orders – Ozzy was sitting on a plane heading for Clarkston, Michigan to resume the Ozzfest tour. As Ozzy himself admitted: 'It lasted a week because I was getting on Sharon's nerves to the point where I'm going, "Are you OK, baby, do you need anything?" And I'm crying, "Oh, my baby".'

When Sharon was rushed back into hospital at the end of August suffering from dehydration – a common side effect of chemotherapy – Ozzy flew back to be with her, but when she was released she once again insisted that he resume the tour. As usual, Ozzy's audiences witnessed the show of a lifetime, but deep inside Ozzy was in pain, his heart elsewhere. He would call Sharon literally dozens of times throughout the day to check that she was alright, and told one audience: 'My spirit's dead,' as he led them in chants of Sharon's name. 'When someone you love is sick, you can't go on stage and pretend you haven't got a broken heart,' he said afterwards. When Ozzfest ended, a grief-stricken Ozzy returned home and with no music to help him through his pain, turned – not for the first time in his life – to the bottle. As Sharon explained: 'What do you do when your wife's in hospital having fucking blood transfusions and you're at home on your own? Any guy would go, "Jesus Christ, I've got to have a drink". And so that's all he had to hang on to, to try to take the pain away. It's really difficult for anyone who's been an addict and an alcoholic their entire life. We try and make light of it, "Oh, dad's an alcoholic, ha ha ha". But it's a terrible thing because it's a disease and it's no different from me having cancer.' In a rare interview, daughter Aimee poignantly explained: 'I don't think he even wants to know what life will be like without her. I don't think he would last more than one year.'

But as Ozzy struggled to come to terms with his wife's illness, Sharon was determined to get on with life and to look on the bright side. Filming for the second series of *The Osbournes* began in the summer and Sharon told MTV that they could cover her chemotherapy treatment to try to help any viewers who might be going through the same thing. 'We want the show to be comic. So if there is anything funny about cancer, we want to find it,' she explained. She was now seeing much more of her seventy-six-year-old father Don and her older brother David, fifty-two. Sharon and Don had been reunited only in November 2001, following their twenty-year feud, but Sharon's illness had inevitably brought them closer together and throughout the summer Don spent much time becoming re-acquainted with his daughter, son-in-law and three grandchildren.

Meanwhile, to cheer himself up, Ozzy decided to splash out on a new house. In addition to his palatial homes in Los Angeles and Buckinghamshire in England, he decided the family also needed a place in New York. After much deliberation, he chose a $6 million (£4 million) luxury apartment with 360-degree views on the forty-eighth floor of Trump Palace, and waited with bated breath as his application was considered. But, to his bitter disappointment, he was turned down. The man whose reputation for biting the head off bats and holding some of the wildest parties in rock checked through the letter to see which particular misdeed from his past had frightened off the Trump Palace grandees, but nothing was listed. The truth, which finally leaked out a few weeks later, was altogether more mundane. 'Their application listed three dogs,' said a Trump Palace insider. 'The building no longer allows new dogs on the premises.' The man with a penchant for sex, drugs and the darker side of life had been rejected simply because of his fondness for cuddly Chihuahuas. Ozzy, predictably, remained sanguine. He would simply stay where he was. 'I would sooner have a roomful of dogs than a roomful of people,' he shrugged.

Not everything was going badly for The Osbournes, however, and Ozzy was delighted – if a little bemused – by daughter Kelly's overnight success as a singer. Her single 'Papa Don't Preach' (a cover of Madonna's 1986 hit) reached Number Three in the British pop charts in September – a higher position than her dad had ever achieved in his musical career – and suddenly the teenager was flavor of the month. She flew to Britain on a promotional tour, appearing on chat shows, giving interviews to magazines and singing on the pop music TV program *Top of the Pops*, a show that her dad had appeared on countless times before she was even born.

Teenage wannabes such as Kelly are usually a godsend to music promoters. They happily do as they are told, smile sweetly and rarely kick up a fuss, unlike seasoned performers who have been round the block a few times. But Kelly was nothing if not her father's child. 'I've got my dad's bad habits,' she admitted. 'The way he eats, and he farts and burps in public and, like him, I often put my foot in my mouth big time.' She had already started dating thrash band singer Bert McCracken and, while she was happy to sing her heart out to promote her single, she was not going to change her rebel image for anyone. On a photo shoot for the American teen magazine *CosmoGirl*, a stylist tried to persuade Kelly to wear a skimpy midriff-revealing top. Kelly's response was typically Osbourne in its bluntness. 'I think you neglected to notice that I'm fat. I'm not going to wear it,' Kelly recounted afterwards. 'She's like, "We'll airbrush it out", I'm like, "Are you nuts?" In the end I put this ugly black t-shirt on with a belt and just stood there.' Rumors, too, filtered out that Kelly had played to the full the part of diva pop star during her appearance on *Top of the Pops*, demanding six dressing rooms, six litres of cola and twelve white towels in each room. But the teenager angrily denied the charges. 'I only had one dressing room and I could touch both walls at the same time. I don't drink cola. I only have bitter lemon and water. And what the fuck would I need a towel for? I only did one song,' she hit back. Meanwhile, American footwear company Candie signed up Kelly to promote their shoes, but her film debut was sadly cut short when she pulled out of the Hollywood movie *Freaky Friday* at the eleventh hour in order to spend more time with her sick mum.

But if Ozzy had hoped that Kelly's success would finally bring peace and harmony to the Osbourne household, he couldn't have been more wrong. Kelly's older sister Aimee had been trying to make her own way in the music business for some time and was working on an album of her own songs. She had considered recording 'Papa Don't Preach' herself, but wasn't ready to release anything, so when Sharon suggested Kelly record the song instead, Aimee agreed that it was an excellent idea. According to Kelly, however, when the song became a hit, everything changed. 'Having a hit is what Aimee really wants and it fell into my lap. She pretends not to be jealous, but when anything good happens to me she gets pissed off and it really hurts my feelings,' Kelly complained. 'It was her idea for me to do the song. Don't tell me to do something if you're going to hate me for it! I don't talk to her about anything I do in music. We argue enough as it is.'

Jack, meanwhile, was enjoying success of his own. Still working as a record company talent scout, the success of *The Osbournes* saw him signed up to film a cameo in the cult teenage television series, *Dawson's Creek*. And although only seventeen he was finding himself, for the first time in his life, in demand with the opposite sex. Girls flocked around him at clubs, and on several occasions he was spotted out on the LA scene with stunning former model and would-be singer Catalina Guirado, several years his senior. Ozzy's family in England were also having a good year. His DJ son Louis signed a deal to record a dance CD, and his estranged daughter, Jessica Hobbs, gave birth to a baby girl, Isabelle – Ozzy's first grandchild. Meanwhile, as far as was possible, Sharon was determined that it should be business as usual. In mid-September, accompanied by daughter Kelly, she made her first public appearance since being diagnosed with cancer in July, to accept an Emmy award for best reality series for *The Osbournes*. Sharon, one of the show's producers, told a cheering audience that she was accepting the award on behalf of her husband, saying, 'Ozzy, I love you'.

Ozzy, inspired by Sharon's courage, decided it was now time to get his life back on an even keel, too, and the following month he decided to try once more to tackle his drinking. He initially hired a sobriety counselor but, not surprisingly, such a new age approach just wasn't Ozzy. After their first yoga session, his counselor read him a poem to calm him down, but Ozzy's response at the end of the reading was typically forthright. 'What the fuck was all that about?' he asked in amazement. Instead, Ozzy announced that he would go cold turkey and detox for two weeks. His doctors, however, warned him that to give up everything – drink and his various prescription drugs in one fell swoop – could be such a shock to his system that it could cause a heart attack or stroke. For safety, doctors decided to put him on a new set of pills that would keep him calm during the detox. But during tests to ascertain a suitable dose, it was discovered that, on top of everything else, he was suffering from abnormally high blood pressure. As ever, Ozzy's health problems were never easy to beat. To add to his misery, his old throat problems had returned. In pain and finding it difficult to speak, he was forced to bow out of a round of interviews to promote *The*

Osbournes show in Britain, leaving them to the rest of the family. Luckily, by the end of the month, Ozzy had recovered sufficiently to appear in concert in Las Vegas, his first solo show since 1997. Sharon knew how much it meant for Ozzy to have her waiting in the wings, telling him what to wear, what to eat and when to rest, and when she announced that she – along with the rest of the family – would be there to support him, Ozzy was delighted. Similarly, Sharon wasn't about to let down Kelly, who celebrated her eighteenth birthday in style at the end of October with a family party organized by her mum at Los Angeles' exclusive Lutece Restaurant. The restaurant is a regular haunt of the rich and famous, but the upmarket clientele had seen nothing like this before. The menu may have consisted of conventional fare – prime rib, shrimp and a two-tiered chocolate cake with pink icing trim – but, to Kelly's delight, Ozzy had laid on a troupe of drag artists to entertain guests for the night, and the highlight of the evening was Kelly and Sharon joining a male Tina Turner impersonator on stage for a raucous rendition of the Prince song 'Star.' Interest in the head of the family meanwhile showed no sign of waning. A major film studio contacted Sharon to say they were interested in making a warts-and-all film of Ozzy's life story. Ozzy wouldn't appear in the movie in person, but top Hollywood actor Johnny Depp was being considered to play the man himself.

If *The Osbournes* had taken America by storm, things were to be no less crazy when the show finally reached terrestrial television in Britain. A lucky few had seen the series via satellite on MTV, but when Channel Four began screening it in November, millions tuned in. The launch was accompanied by a $750,000 (£500,000) advertising campaign: giant billboard posters appeared of Ozzy, with quotes from the show, such as 'It could be worse, I could be ******* Sting.' In addition there were TV spots, a national radio campaign and an eight-page color booklet – filled with pictures and Ozzy's pearls of wisdom – which was given away free with newspapers and magazines. Ozzy, as ever, was baffled by the attention. 'You get out of bed, you scratch your balls, you have a shower, and then you go about your day. The show hasn't changed my life, because I don't know what I'm doing anyway,' he said.

On the evening of 26 November, 6.6 million viewers across America sat down in front of their television screens for the much-awaited launch of the second series of *The Osbournes*. In the first episode Ozzy is seen practising yoga on his tour bus during Ozzfest, but if the sight of their hero in such a calm pose gave viewers the impression he had gone soft and run out of antics to shock and amuse them, they need not have worried. Later in the same episode the cameras cut to a shot of Ozzy taking his screeching pet bird and putting its head right inside his mouth. The bird lived to see another day and afterwards, by way of explanation, Ozzy bizarrely insisted that he had only been trying to calm it down! Delighted MTV bosses announced that ratings for the first episode were up eighty-four per cent on the first season's opening night. MTV Entertainment President Brian Graden said proudly: 'The Osbournes' juggernaut shows little sign of slowing down.' To the Osbourne children, however, their new-found fame was still difficult to fathom. 'Maybe it's because we're not that different and we're not full of shit. But I don't understand it, to be totally honest,' pondered Kelly. Jack meanwhile described the show as no more than a 'home video'. 'Everyone thinks you have this grand lifestyle, with champagne, water fountains, gold-plated bathtubs. Then they realize that Dad and Mom and all of us are a regular family, and they relate to our issues,' he said.

But just like their Dad, the children couldn't always be trusted to behave, and MTV executives were suddenly put on the spot twice. First Kelly and Jack claimed that two key scenes from the first series had been faked. They cited two specific moments – the appearance of a dog therapist and a dramatic family meeting that ended with Jack storming out. 'The most fake thing about that show was the family meeting, because that was an MTV idea,' said Kelly. 'The dog and the dog therapist, that was an MTV thing. I put in my contract for the new series that I would not do anything like that fucking dog therapist.' Ironically, for a man who had spent his entire youth causing headaches for his parents, it was an embarrassed Ozzy's turn to clear up after his own children and he was forced to issue a swift denial. 'Ozzy and Sharon would not have done it unless it were all real,' his spokesman insisted. As if that weren't bad enough, Kelly then slammed the series as 'retarded'. 'If I'm in a bad mood in one episode, I'm considered a bitch for the rest of my life,' she said. 'I don't want to do any more. If they offered me $100 million (£66 million) I wouldn't do it.' Sharon, too, hinted that despite lucrative offers, the second series would be their last. She said the show had changed them all and that Kelly and Jack now had their own lawyers and business managers – Jack even had his own bodyguard after being attacked in a nightclub – and that they had all been innocent about what to expect when they began. 'We went in feet first and you can't recreate that,' she explained. 'This series, people will see what the first series has done to our lives and it will take people on to the next stage. But after that, it's over.' Off-screen the family agreed to take in Kelly's best friend Robert Marcato, eighteen, whose own mother has just recently died of colon cancer, the same disease that Sharon was suffering from. He was immediately dubbed 'Baby Osbourne' and it was agreed that once he settled in to the family he would become part of the show. Kelly said: 'My mum loves him like her own. He's been so amazing with her.' Explained Sharon: 'I treat him no differently than my own kids. So obviously I swear at him.'

Meanwhile Ozzymania continued apace and, as the second series became cult viewing across the States, shops were soon stacked full of Ozzy merchandise. For Ozzy, who had only ever wanted to sell records, it was bewildering to walk into a store to be confronted by Ozzy dolls, pens, piggy banks, mugs bearing the slogan, 'The Osbournes – The Parents You Wish You Had' and even an Osbournes Snow Globe featuring 'The Blizzard of Oz' amidst a generous sprinkling of stars, snow and bats. But despite the success, Ozzy was still struggling to cope with Sharon's illness. His big, bad, wild-man-of-rock image was mostly all show. Without Sharon to support him, he found life difficult, and the thought of living without her would frequently reduce him to floods of uncontrollable tears. In November he broke down during an interview on American television with chat show host Barbara Walters when he was asked what Sharon meant to him. 'She's the greatest love I've ever had in my life. She's my pillar of strength and hope,' he sobbed. 'I'm absolutely horrified. It's the worst thing that could ever happen.' Echoing Ozzy's feelings, Kelly told the same show that she feared for the future of the whole family if Sharon failed to pull through. 'It would fall apart,' she said bleakly. 'We couldn't go on without her. Out of everyone in my whole life, if I ever lost my mother I think I'd kill myself. I couldn't live without her.'

In December Kelly was in the news again with the video she had made to accompany her second single 'Shut Up', taken from the album of the same name. What Ozzy didn't know until it was finished – and then too late to change – was that his youngest daughter had used the video to make fun of his most infamous moment, dressing herself in a black outfit and wig and playfully gnawing the head off a chocolate bat on a stick. Christmas, as usual, was spent at the family home in Beverly Hills and, as usual, it was a chaotic affair. Ozzy and the clan had generously offered to help out at a shelter for the homeless on Christmas Eve, but just twenty-four hours later the Christmas cheer had disappeared – normal service had been resumed. The family managed a traditional festive dinner, complete with Sharon's homemade roast potatoes, and the head of the household proudly carved the turkey. Ozzy was thrilled to receive a first edition copy of *Dracula* from Sharon, but as he admitted afterwards: 'It was the usual bloody nightmare – arguments, too much food, screaming matches and the rest. But that's fucking Christmas for you. It's a family time, isn't it?'

Back in Britain, millions were sharing their own Christmas Day with the Osbourne clan. Sharon, to her amazement, had been asked to record an Alternative Christmas Message to be shown on Channel Four at 3pm – exactly the same time as the Queen's traditional message to the nation was being screened on BBC1. Just like the Queen, Sharon was filmed in her own home; just like the Queen, she was dressed in her finest; just like the Queen, she talked glowingly about the achievements of her family; and just like the Queen, she had her pet dogs around her (although the royal corgis have never been filmed wearing toy antlers). Sharon hadn't disgraced herself once. As the credits started to roll, the film crew looked on in disbelief. What had happened to the Osbourne spirit? With just seconds to go, the cameras panned back one final time for a close-up of Sharon cuddling the dogs under the tree. She looked up and grinned. 'Fucking Happy Christmas,' she yelled before breaking out into a raucous laugh. Watching from the wings, Ozzy let out a huge cheer – she hadn't let him down after all. Explaining their decision to invite her to make the broadcast, a Channel Four spokeswoman said: 'Sharon Osbourne connects with our viewers in a way that the Queen can't. She is a real person who leads an extraordinary life.'

Despite the agonies they had been through with Sharon's illness, 2002 ended on a high for the Osbournes; they were told that cancer was no longer detectable in Sharon's blood tests and that the chemotherapy treatment, which had been scheduled until April, would now more than likely end in February. Said Ozzy: 'It's getting easier to banish dark thoughts.'

Meanwhile, the famous couple decided to end the year in style, with a lavish $750,000 (£500,000) party at the Beverly Hills hotel, to celebrate the renewal of their wedding vows made twenty years earlier. The New Year's Eve extravaganza was shown live on MTV. Aimee was maid of honor and Jack was best man. Kelly was flower girl – she said later: 'I had to wear a frilly frock and throw rose petals down to make a red carpet. Mum was crying before she even walked down the aisle, but I didn't cry because I was too busy laughing.' Sharon, dressed in a cream gown and tiara, was walked down the petal-strewn aisle by her father, Don. For the first time anyone could remember, Ozzy donned a tie and smart black Armani suit and, in a moving ceremony, the couple read out vows they had written themselves, before kissing passionately in front of the 200 guests, who included singers Justin Timberlake and Marilyn Manson, US comedian Chris Rock and the family's assorted doctors. The touching ceremony had been due to take place on the couple's twentieth anniversary in July, but had been delayed because of Sharon's battle against cancer, and both Sharon and Ozzy fought back tears as she told him: 'I'm privileged to be your wife. I love you, thank you for my babies.' The ceremony was conducted by Rabbi Steven Rubin – in recognition of Sharon's Jewish roots – who told them: 'The love that sparkles between you is without question the greatest gift life has to offer.' Then he produced two glasses of wine to be sipped during the recitation of blessings. 'Is this real wine?' asked Ozzy, with a huge grin on his face. 'Yes, it is,' retorted the rabbi. 'Hold it away from your clothes.'

The ceremony may have been moving, but Ozzy hadn't gone soft in his old age, and as soon as the formalities were over the party began Ozzy-style. Six Royal guards – in fact actors wearing Household Cavalry uniforms – directed guests through to the Sunset Ballroom where performing midgets and strippers mingled with the celebrity guests. A Playboy model, covered only in body paint, danced inside a giant champagne glass, while African drummers and camp 1970s pop stars The Village People provided the entertainment. A paperboy on an antique bicycle handed out copies of a special newspaper full of stories and pictures about the Osbournes and their pets, while guests received goodie bags crammed with gifts from Sharon's favorite stores, including Saks Fifth Avenue and Tiffany's. At midnight, a hologram talking head counted down the seconds as Ozzy and Sharon sat on thrones on a balcony above the Ballroom to receive the raucous cheers of the guests below. Every guest was handed a special condom-shaped lollipop with the words, 'Ozzy and Sharon's renewal of wedding vows' engraved on the side. At Sharon's insistence, the gathering may have had more style than the parties of Ozzy's youth, but for Ozzy a proper party had to include a little bit of mischief.

It was a fitting end to a remarkable year. To cap it all, Ozzy's performance at Buckingham Palace had been voted Number Three in a British poll of events that 'made people smile most' during the year, and an Internet poll named him as the favorite amongst the British public to be made a 'Sir' in the New Year's Honors List – for his services to Friday night television and the 'F' word. Finally, 2002 had left Ozzy rich beyond his wildest dreams. On top of the millions the family were paid for the two series of *The Osbournes*, DVD, video, merchandising and marketing deals had pushed his earnings for the year to more than $20 million (£17 million) – his most lucrative twelve months ever. The family were also signed up to advertise Pepsi With a Twist. The hilarious commercial, screened on television for the first time in the run-up to the American Super Bowl in January, shows Jack and Kelly transformed into squeaky-clean Donny and Marie Osmond, and Ozzy waking in bed from this nightmare to find Sharon replaced by the Brady Bunch's clean-living Carol Brady.

Yet, despite it all, none of his newfound glory seems to have changed him, nor is it likely to do so. At the American Music Awards in Los Angeles in January, which the Osbournes had been asked to co-host, American TV censors were left working overtime to bleep out the bad language during the live broadcast. Sharon was the first to offend, introducing singer Mariah Carey with the words, 'She sings like a mother-fucker, I fucking love her', but Ozzy typically wasn't far behind, leaving the audience in stitches as he immediately apologized: 'You can't take the fucking lady anywhere anymore!'

Ozzy has always been one of those people who stumble through life without a plan, falling headfirst into every mess they come across, but somehow still managing to come up smelling of roses. There are rumors that he will take time out in 2003 to record an album of cover versions, and an even more extraordinary suggestion that he will team up with Australian singer Kylie Minogue to sing 'Especially For You', the romantic duet she originally sang with *Neighbours* co-star Jason Donovan in 1989. As ever, there will be Ozzfest in the summer and there are still hopes for a third series of *The Osbournes*, despite Sharon and Kelly's firm denials.

Instead, the couple may consider a $15 million (£10 million) offer to turn *The Osbournes* into a *Simpsons*-style cartoon. Sharon, meanwhile, has signed a deal with Warner Bros to host her own daytime US TV chat show in the autumn.

But beyond that – unsurprisingly – there are no plans. What we can be sure of is that, having lived such an extraordinary life so far, Ozzy will continue to do just that. He still struggles with his addictions and there is little reason to think anything will ever be any different. 'The only time I really feel comfortable in my own skin is when I'm drinking or taking pills,' he admits. 'You know the *Wizard of Oz*, when they get to the end, and there's this wimpy man behind the curtain? That's how I feel. This big persona, this flaming demon, and I'm this little man.' Many of his contemporaries who lived those wild times alongside him have fallen by the wayside, several dying tragically through drink or drugs overdoses, others falling into ill health, middle-age and obscurity. Those who have survived have invariably descended into the self-parody so beloved of aging rock stars. Ozzy, now fifty-four, lived life faster and harder than all of them, but has somehow avoided this fate. He did it all wrong, but somehow ended up doing it all right.

Whether it is charisma, talent, good management or simply good luck, something has carried Ozzy through the past turbulent half-century and into the extraordinary position he now finds himself in today. As the legend himself says: 'I'm a lucky man. I realize it. There's always someone out there greater than me; I just had a great break and if it all goes down the shit-pan, then I can't complain. Everything comes to an end, sooner or later, I suppose. But the truth is, I don't want it to end. I mean, what the fuck does a lunatic do when he retires?'

Ozzy Osbourne: Discography and Videos

7-inch and 12-inch singles, CD singles and CD maxi-singles chronologically

1969 Wicked World / Evil Woman: UK 7-inch single

1970 Evil Woman / Wicked World: UK 7-inch single; silver & swirl labels

1970 Paranoid / The Wizard: UK & US 7-inch single; silver & swirl labels

1970 Paranoid: US 10-inch acetate

1970 Paranoid: UK 12-inch single; clear vinyl; picture sleeve

1972 Tomorrow's Dream / Laguna Sunrise: UK 7-inch single; silver & swirl labels

1973 Paranoid / Sabbath Bloody Sabbath; Tomorrow's Dream / Changes: Australian double 7-inch single; picture sleeve

1973 Sabbath Bloody Sabbath / Changes: UK & US 7-inch single

1973 Looking For Today / Sabbath Bloody Sabbath/ Sabbra Cadabra: US 7-inch EP; picture sleeve

1974 Iron Man / Electric Funeral: US 7-inch single

1975 Am I Going Insane (Radio) / Hole In The Sky: UK 7-inch single

1975 Paranoid / Iron Man: US 7-inch single

1976 Paranoid / Evil Woman: Australian 7-inch single

1977 Paranoid / Sabbath Bloody Sabbath: UK 7-inch single

1978 Paranoid / Snowblind: UK 7-inch single

1978 Hard Road / Symptom Of The Universe: UK 7-inch single; limited edition on purple vinyl

1978 Never Say Die / She's Gone: UK 7-inch single; tan & blue labels; limited-edition picture sleeve

1980 Crazy Train / You Looking At Me Looking At You: UK & US 7-inch single

1980 Mr. Crowley / You Said It All (Live): UK & US 7-inch single

1980 Live EP: Mr. Crowley / You Said It All (Live) / Suicide Solution (Live): UK & US 12-inch single; Canadian edition on black vinyl; UK picture sleeve; limited-edition picture disk

1981 Flying High Again / I Don't Know (Live): US 7-inch single

1981 Crazy Train / Steal Away (The Night): US 7-inch single

1981 Over The Mountain / I Don't Know: UK & US 7-inch & 12-inch single

1982 Little Dolls / Tonight: UK & US 7-inch single

1982 Never Say Die (Live) / Paranoid (Live): US 7-inch single; both tracks from *Speak Of The Devil* (see p. 195)

1982 Symptom Of The Universe / N.I.B: UK 7-inch single; picture disk; both tracks from *Speak Of The Devil*

1982 Symptom Of The Universe / Iron Man / Children Of The Grave: UK 12-inch single; all tracks from *Speak Of The Devil*

1983 Bark At The Moon / One Up The B Side: UK 7-inch single

1983 Bark At The Moon / Spiders: US 7-inch single

1983 Bark At The Moon / One Up The B Side / Slow Down: UK 12-inch single

1983 So Tired / One Up The B Side: US 7-inch single

1984 So Tired / Bark At The Moon (Live): UK 7-inch single; recorded in Salt Lake City, Utah, 18 March 1984

1984 So Tired / Forever (Live): UK 7-inch single

1984 So Tired / Bark At The Moon (Live); Waiting For Darkness / Paranoid (Live): US double 7-inch single; gatefold packaging; recorded in Salt Lake City, Utah, 18 March 1984

1984 So Tired / Waiting For Darkness / Bark At The Moon (Live) / Suicide Solution (Live) / Paranoid (Live): UK 12-inch single; recorded in Salt Lake City, Utah, 18 March 1984; with Ozzy Osbourne logo patch; limited edition on gold vinyl

1986 Shot In The Dark / Rock 'N' Roll Rebel: UK 7-inch single; packaged in a poster bag

1986 Shot In The Dark / Killer Of Giants / Rock 'N' Roll Rebel: UK 12-inch single

1986 Shot In The Dark / Crazy Train: US 7-inch single; reissued by Collectable Records

1986 Shot In The Dark / You Said It All (Live): US 7-inch single

1986 The Ultimate Sin / Lightning Strikes: UK 7-inch single; Castle Donington Festival limited-edition souvenir

1986 *The Ultimate Live Ozzy*: The Ultimate Sin / Never Know Why / Thank God For The Bomb: US 12-inch single; picture disk; limited edition; recorded Kansas City, 1986; live tracks from *The Ultimate Ozzy* video shoot

1987 Close My Eyes Forever (with Lita Ford) / Lita Ford: Under The Gun: UK 7-inch single

1987 Crazy Train (Live from *Tribute*) / Crazy Train (*Blizzard Of Ozz* Version): UK 7-inch & 12-inch single

1987 Crazy Train (Live from *Tribute*) / Crazy Train / I Don't Know: UK 12-inch single; tracks 2 & 3 from *Blizzard Of Ozz*

1988 Close My Eyes Forever (Remix) (with Lita Ford) / Lita Ford: Under The Gun / Blueberry: UK 12-inch picture disk & CD single; Ozzy does not perform on B-side

1988 *Back To Ozz*: The Ultimate Sin / Bark At The Moon / Mr. Crowley (Live EP Version) / Diary Of A Madman: UK 7-inch, 12-inch & CD single; includes color poster with photos and family tree

1988 Miracle Man / Crazy Babies: UK 7-inch single

1988 Miracle Man / You Said It All: US 7-inch single

1988 Miracle Man / Demon Alcohol: US 7-inch single

1988 Miracle Man / Crazy Babies: UK 12-inch single; picture disk shaped like Ozzy's head with a crown of thorns

1988 Crazy Babies / Demon Alcohol: US 7-inch single

1988 Miracle Man / The Liar / Crazy Babies: UK 12-inch single

1988 Led Clones / Speak For Yourself (Ozzy on backup only): US 7-inch single

1990 *Just Say Ozzy*: Miracle Man / Bloodbath In Paradise / Shot In The Dark / Tattooed Dancer / Sweet Leaf / War Pigs: UK & US 7-inch, cassette & CD single; live EP from No Rest tour. 1995 reissued as digitally remastered CD single

1990 The Urpney Song (with Frank Bruno and Billy Connolly) / The Whirlyped Launch: UK 7-inch single; from animated TV series for Central TV, UK; Ozzy does not perform on B-side

1991 Mama, I'm Coming Home / Don't Blame Me: UK 7-inch single; jukebox only

1991 Mama, I'm Coming Home (Special Version) / Goodbye To Romance / Time After Time: UK 12-inch single

1991 Mama, I'm Coming Home (Special Version) / Don't Blame Me / I Don't Know / Crazy Train: UK 12-inch single

1991 Mama, I'm Coming Home / Don't Blame Me / Party With The Animals: US CD maxi-single

1991 Alice Cooper: Hey Stoopid / Wind-Up Toy: UK & US 7-inch single; Ozzy sings backup on A-side

1991 No More Tears / S.I.N: UK 7-inch single

1991 No More Tears / S.I.N. / Party With The Animals: UK 12-inch & CD single; 12-inch was picture disk; CD single in embossed wallet; each sleeve has a different picture; Party With The Animals from soundtrack of *Buffy the Vampire Slayer*

1991 No More Tears / S.I.N. / Don't Blame Me / Party With The Animals: US CD maxi-single; track 3 as above

1992 Shake Your Head / Was (Not Was) (with Kim Basinger): US 12-inch single

1993 Changes / No More Tears: UK 7-inch single

1993 Changes / No More Tears /

Desire / Changes (with Audience): UK 12-inch & CD single; 12-inch was picture disk

1995 Perry Mason (Edit) / Living With The Enemy: UK 7-inch single; numbered, limited-edition picture disk

1995 Perry Mason (Edit) / Perry Mason (Album Version) / Living With The Enemy / The Whole World's Falling Down: UK CD single

1995 DISK 1: Perry Mason (Edit) / Living With The Enemy / The Whole World's Falling Down DISK 2: Perry Mason (Album Version) / No More Tears / I Don't Want To Change The World / Flying High Again: UK CD singles in double-pack

1996 See You On The Other Side (Edit) / See You On The Other Side (Album Version) / Voodoo Dancer / Aimee: UK CD single

1996 I Just Want You (Album Version) / Aimee (Rough Demo) / Voodoo Dancer (Rough Demo): UK 12-inch single; B-side has an etched 'Best Wishes Ozzy Osbourne' in Ozzy's own 'handwriting', plus Ozzy sketch

1996 DISK 1: I Just Want You (Single Edit) / Aimee / Mama, I'm Coming Home DISK 2: I Just Want You (Single Edit) / Voodoo Dancer (Rough Demo) / Iron Man (*Nativity In Black* Version): UK 2 CD singles in double-pack

1996 I Just Want You (Mixes); Aimee; Voodoo Dancer; Mama, I'm Coming Home; Iron Man: UK CD single; two versions issued on same day with different catalog numbers

1997 Back On Earth / Walk On Water / I Just Want You: UK CD single

1998 *Ozzfest Doggy Bag (Choice Cuts To Snack On Later)*: Black Sabbath: Snowblind (Live 1997, previously unreleased): US PC-enhanced CD single; includes Incubus Mustached Mystic / UFO shooting game

1998 Black Sabbath: Psycho Man: US CD single

1999 Buried Alive (Radio) / Buried Alive (Full): UK CD single

1999 *97.7 FM Interviews*: Interview 3 November 1992 / Interview October 1995 / Interview November 1997: US CD single

1999 *Black Mass*: Paranoid; Black Sabbath; Iron Man; Blue Suede Shoes: UK & US CD maxi-single; Black Sabbath EP

1999 Interview Disk – Black Sabbath: UK & US CD single

2000 *Coal Chamber: The Monkey*: US CD single
Shock The Monkey / Shock The Monkey (Gorilla Mix) / El Cuy Cuy (Alternate Mix); Ozzy guests

2001 Gets Me Through: UK CD single

2001 *Ozz Talk*: US CD maxi-single; interviews

2001 Gets Me Through (Edit) / No Place For Angels / Alive: UK & US CD single

2002 Dreamer: UK CD single

2002 Dreamer: US PC-enhanced CD maxi-single

2002 Dreamer / Gets Me Through: UK & US CD single

2002 Dreamer (Album Version) / Gets Me Through (Radio Edit) / Black Skies / Dreamer (Video): UK & US CD single

2002 Dreamer (Album Version) / Black Skies (Non-LP) / Dreamer (Acoustic) / Dreamer (Enhanced Video): UK & US PC-enhanced CD single

Vinyl, cassette and CD albums chronologically

1970 *Black Sabbath*: UK LP; N.I.B. refers to the nickname the band had for Bill Ward's beard – 'pen nib'.
Black Sabbath; The Wizard; Wasp / Behind The Wall Of Sleep; Basically / N.I.B.; Evil Woman; A Bit Of Finger / Sleeping Village; Warning

1970 *Black Sabbath*: US LP. The Wizard; Wasp / Behind The Wall Of Sleep; Basically / N.I.B.; Wicked World; A Bit Of Finger / Sleeping Village; Warning

1970 *Paranoid*: UK & US LP; 1976 limited-edition picture disk; 1980 issued on cassette & CD; 1996 digitally remastered CD reissue; 2000 limited-edition reissue replicates original LP packaging in a cardboard digipak; album was originally to be called *War Pigs*.
Luke's Wall / War Pigs; Paranoid; Planet Caravan; Iron Man; Electric Funeral; Hand Of Doom; Rat Salad; Fairies Wear Boots / Jack The Stripper

1971 *Master of Reality*: UK & US LP; 1980 issued on cassette & CD; 1996 digitally remastered CD reissue; 2000 limited-edition reissue replicates original LP packaging in a cardboard digipak.
Sweet Leaf; After Forever; Embryo; Children Of The Grave; Orchid; Lord Of This World; Solitude; Into The Void

1972 *Volume 4*: UK & US LP; 1980 issued on cassette & CD; 1996 digitally remastered CD reissued; 2000 limited-edition reissue replicates original LP packaging in a cardboard digipak; album was originally to be called *Snowblind*.
Wheels Of Confusion / The Straightener; Tomorrow's Dream; Changes; FX; Supernaut; Snowblind; Cornucopia; Laguna Sunrise; St. Vitus' Dance; Under The Sun / Every Day Comes & Goes

1973 *Sabbath Bloody Sabbath*: UK & US LP; 1980 issued on cassette & CD; 1996 digitally remastered CD reissued; 2000 limited-edition reissue replicates original LP packaging in a cardboard digipak.

Sabbath Bloody Sabbath; A National Acrobat; Fluff; Sabbra Cadabra; Killing Yourself To Live; Who Are You?; Looking For Today; Spiral Architect

1975 *Sabotage*: UK & US LP & cassette; 1980 issued on CD; 1996 digitally remastered CD reissued; 2000 limited-edition reissue replicates original LP packaging in a cardboard digipak; bonus on some editions is 23-second song as part of The Writ (recorded at very low volume) called Blow On A Jug.

Hole In The Sky; Don't Start (Too Late); Symptom Of The Universe; Megalomania; The Thrill Of It All; Supertzar; Am I Going Insane (Radio); The Writ

1975 *We Sold Our Soul For Rock & Roll*: UK & US double LP & cassette; 1986 issued on CD; 1996 digitally remastered CD reissued; 2000 limited-edition reissue replicates original LP packaging in a cardboard digipak; Warning and Laguna Sunrise were left off the first CD release; tracks restored in 1996.

Black Sabbath; The Wizard; Paranoid; War Pigs; Iron Man; Tomorrow's Dream; Fairies Wear Boots; Changes; Sweet Leaf; Children Of The Grave; Sabbath Bloody Sabbath; Am I Going Insane (Radio); Snowblind; N.I.B.; Warning; Laguna Sunrise

1976 *Technical Ecstasy*: UK & US LP & cassette; 1980 issued on CD; 1996 CD digitally remastered; 2000 limited-edition reissue replicates original LP packaging in a cardboard digipak; Ozzy left and rejoined Black Sabbath between this album and the next. Back Street Kids; You Won't Change Me; It's Alright; Gypsy; All Moving Parts (Stand Still); Rock 'N' Roll Doctor; She's Gone; Dirty Women

1978 *Never Say Die*: UK & US LP &

cassette; 1980 issued on CD; 2000 limited-edition reissue replicates original LP packaging in a cardboard digipak; Ozzy's last album with Black Sabbath. Never Say Die; Johnny Blade; Junior's Eyes; A Hard Road; Shock Wave; Air Dance; Over To You; Breakout; Swinging The Chain

1980 *Black Sabbath*: UK & US reissued on cassette & CD; bonus track

1980 Black Sabbath: *Greatest Hits*: UK & US LP, cassette & CD; 1986 reissued with bonus track After Forever. Paranoid; N.I.B.; Changes; Sabbath Bloody Sabbath; Iron Man; Black Sabbath; War Pigs; Laguna Sunrise; Tomorrow's Dream; Sweet Leaf

1980 *Blizzard Of Ozz*: UK & US LP, cassette & CD; Ozzy's first solo record; the English pressing has a different back cover. 1996 digitally remastered CD reissued with Internet interaction. I Don't Know; Crazy Train; Goodbye To Romance; Dee; Suicide Solution; Mr. Crowley; No Bone Movies; Revelation (Mother Earth); Steal Away (The Night)

1981 *Diary Of A Madman*: UK & US LP, cassette & CD; recorded with *Blizzard of Ozz*; 1996 digitally remastered CD reissued. Over The Mountain; Flying High Again; You Can't Kill Rock 'N' Roll; Believer; Little Dolls; Tonight; S.A.T.O.; Diary Of A Madman

1982 *Speak Of The Devil*: UK & US double LP, cassette & CD; recorded at the Ritz Club, New York, on 26–7 September 1982; original US CD omitted Sweet Leaf; titled *Talk of the Devil* in UK and Europe. Released to fulfill a contact for a live album for the Diary of a Madman tour. Randy Rhoads died in a plane crash

during the tour and Ozzy felt he would be exploiting Randy's name by releasing the original album.
Symptom Of The Universe; Snowblind; Black Sabbath; Fairies Wear Boots; War Pigs; The Wizard; N.I.B.; Sweet Leaf; Never Say Die; Sabbath Bloody Sabbath; Iron Man; Children Of The Grave; Paranoid

1983 *Bark At The Moon*: UK LP, cassette & CD; 1996 digitally remastered CD reissued.
Bark At The Moon; You're No Different; Now You See It (Now You Don't); Rock 'N' Roll Rebel; Forever; So Tired; Slow Down; Waiting For Darkness

1983 *Bark At The Moon*: US LP, cassette & CD; this edition has Slow Down instead of Spiders; also Forever is listed as Center of Eternity; songs are in a different order. 1996 digitally remastered CD reissued with bonus track Spiders

1983 *Was (Not Was)*: *Born to Laugh At Tornadoes*: US LP, cassette & CD; Ozzy sings on one track.
Shake Your Head, Let's Go To Bed (Version 1)

1983 *Paranoid / Heaven & Hell*: US cassette & CD; reissue of the two LPs

1986 *The Ultimate Sin*: UK & US LP, cassette & CD; 1996 digitally remastered CD reissued.
The Ultimate Sin; Secret Loser; Never Know Why; Thank God For The Bomb; Lightning Strikes; Never; Killer Of Giants; Fool Like You; Shot In The Dark

1987 Lita Ford: *Lita*: US LP, cassette & CD; also on LP entitled *The Best Of Lita Ford*; Ozzy sings on one track.
Close My Eyes Forever (with Lita Ford)

1987 *Tribute*: UK & US LP, cassette & CD; 2002 digitally remastered CD reissued; uniquely listed as Ozzy Osbourne / Randy Rhoads.

I Don't Know; Crazy Train; Believer; Mr. Crowley; Flying High Again; Revelation (Mother Earth); Steal Away (The Night); Suicide Solution (with guitar solo); Iron Man; Children Of The Grave; Paranoid; Goodbye To Romance; No Bone Movies; Dee (Randy Rhoads's studio outtakes)

1988 *No Rest For The Wicked*: UK & US LP, cassette & CD; CD and cassette have an unlisted bonus track Hero. 1996 digitally remastered CD reissued.
Miracle Man; Devil's Daughter; Crazy Babies; Breaking All The Rules; Bloodbath In Paradise; Fire In The Sky; Tattooed Dancer; Demon Alcohol

1988 Gary Moore: *After the War*: US LP, cassette & CD; Ozzy sings backup / harmony on one track.
Speak For Yourself

1989 Black Sabbath: *Blackest Sabbath*: UK & US CD; greatest-hits compilation; Ozzy only sings on some tracks.
Black Sabbath; Paranoid; Iron Man; Snowblind; Sabbath Bloody Sabbath; Hole In The Sky; Rock 'N' Roll Doctor; Never Say Die; Lady Evil; Turn Up The Night; Sign Of The Southern Cross; Heaven And Hell (Live); Children Of The Sea; Digital Bitch; Seventh Star; Born To Lose

1989 Make A Difference Foundation: *Stairway to Heaven / Highway To Hell*: US LP, cassette, CD; all of the songs on this record were originally written by bands that have been touched by drug or alcohol problems. Ozzy sings on one track with Zakk Wylde, Randy Castillo, Geezer Butler.
Purple Haze

1990 *The Dreamstone*: UK LP, cassette & CD; from animated TV series for Central TV, UK; Ozzy sings on one track.
The Urpney Song (with Frank Bruno and Billy Connolly)

1990 Bill Ward: *Ward One: Along the Way*: US LP, cassette & CD; Ozzy sings two songs.
Bombers (Can Open Bomb Bays) / Jack's Land

1990 *Ten Commandments*: UK & US cassette & CD; limited collector's edition.
Flying High Again; Crazy Train; Diary Of A Madman; Shot In The Dark; Thank God For The Bomb; Bark At The Moon; Tonight; Little Dolls; Steal Away (The Night); So Tired

1991 *Talk of the Devil*: UK CD; reissued under European name with digital remastering; bonus track Sweet Leaf

1991 Alice Cooper: *Hey Stoopid*: US LP, cassette & CD; Ozzy sings backup on one track.
Hey Stoopid

1991 Infectious Grooves: *The Plague That Makes Your Booty Move*: US cassette & CD; Ozzy sings on one track.
Therapy

1991 *No More Tears*: UK LP, UK & US cassette & CD; reissue with digital remastering.
Mr. Tinkertrain; I Don't Want To Change The World; Mama, I'm Coming Home; Desire; No More Tears; S.I.N.; Hellraiser; Time After Time; Zombie Stomp; A.V.H.; Road To Nowhere

1992 Motörhead: *March or Die*: UK & US LP, cassette & CD; Ozzy sings on one track.
I Ain't No Nice Guy (with Lemmy)

1992 Was (Not Was): *Hello Dad . . . I'm in Jail*: US cassette & CD; Ozzy sings on one track.
Shake Your Head, Let's Go To Bed (Version 2)

1992 *Buffy The Vampire Slayer*: UK & US cassette & CD; from soundtrack; Ozzy sings on one track.
Party With The Animals

1993 *Live & Loud*: UK double-LP, UK & US double cassette & CD; from No More Tours tour; limited-edition double CD in digipak with speaker-grille front, booklet and two tattoo transfers; 1996 digitally remastered CD reissued in double jewel case without transfers.
Intro; Paranoid; I Don't Want To Change The World; Desire; Mr. Crowley; I Don't Know; Road To Nowhere; Flying High Again; Guitar Solo; Suicide Solution; Goodbye To Romance; Shot In The Dark; No More Tears; Miracle Man; Drum Solo; War Pigs; Bark At The Moon; Mama, I'm Coming Home; Crazy Train; Black Sabbath; Changes

1993 *Loud and Proud*: US cassette & CD; heavy-metal compilation; Ozzy sings on one track.
Paranoid

1993 *Dazed And Confused*: US cassette & CD; heavy-metal compilation; Ozzy sings on one track.
Paranoid

1993 *Monsters Of Rock Vol. 1 – Heaven And Hell*: US cassette & CD; heavy-metal compilation; Ozzy sings on one track.
The Ultimate Sin

1994 *Nativity In Black*: UK LP, UK & US cassette & CD; Black Sabbath tribute; Ozzy sings on one track. Also available in a two-CD edition called *The Bible According to Black Sabbath, Old and New Testaments*. *The Old Testament* (Disk 1) has the tribute's songs as performed by Black Sabbath. *The New Testament* (Disk 2) is actual tribute.
Iron Man

1994 *Kermit Unpigged*: US LP, cassette & CD; recorded for an episode of *The Muppet Show*; Ozzy sings on one track.
Born To Be Wild (with Miss Piggy)

1994 Black Sabbath: *Iron Man*: UK & US cassette & CD; greatest-hits compilation.
Sabbath Bloody Sabbath; Wizard;

Sweet Leaf; Electric Funeral; Into The Void; Wheels Of Confusion; Paranoid; Iron Man; Am I Going Insane (Radio); Killing Yourself To Live; Snowblind; Hole In The Sky; Laguna Sunrise; War Pigs

1995 *Ozzmosis*: UK LP, UK & US cassette & CD; 1999 reissued as MiniDisc.
Perry Mason; I Just Want You; Ghost Behind My Eyes; Thunder Underground; See You On The Other Side; Tomorrow; Denial; My Little Man; My Jekyll Doesn't Hide; Old L.A. Tonight

1995 Black Sabbath: *Between Heaven and Hell 1970–1983*: UK & US cassette & CD; greatest-hits compilation.
Hole In The Sky; Into The Void; Sabbath Bloody Sabbath; N.I.B.; Paranoid; War Pigs; Iron Man; Wicked World; Supernaut; Back Street Kids; Never Say Die; Neon Knights; The Mob Rules; The Dark / Zero The Hero; Black Sabbath

1995 *Best Ballads*: CD; Russian compilation.
See You On The Other Side; Mama, I'm Coming Home; Revelation (Mother Earth); Killer Of Giants; Time After Time; Ghost Behind My Eyes; You're No Different; Fire In The Sky; Tonight; Old L.A. Tonight; So Tired; Goodbye To Romance; Road To Nowhere; Close My Eyes Forever

1996 Black Sabbath: *Children of the Grave*: US cassette & CD; digitally remastered version of *Volume 4* with bonus track Children Of The Grave (Live)

1996 *Black Sabbath*: UK & US cassette & CD; reissue of digitally remastered CD.
Black Sabbath; The Wizard; Behind The Wall Of Sleep; N.I.B.; Evil Woman; Sleeping Village; Warning; Wicked World

1996 Black Sabbath: *Greatest Hits*:

UK & US cassette & CD.
Perry Mason; Mr. Tinkertrain; Miracle Man; No More Tears; Bark At The Moon; Crazy Babies; The Ultimate Sin; Never Know Why; I Just Want You; Believer; Mr. Crowley; Thunder Underground; Over The Mountain; Forever

1996 *Beavis and Butt-Head Do America*: US cassette & CD; from soundtrack; Ozzy sings on one track.
Walk On Water

1996 Black Sabbath: *Live At Last*: UK & US cassette & CD; greatest-hits compilation; all tracks digitally remastered.
Tomorrow's Dream; Sweet Leaf; Killing Yourself To Live; Cornucopia; Snowblind; Children Of The Grave; War Pigs; Wicked World; Paranoid

1997 *The Ozzfest Live*: UK LP, UK & US cassette & CD; live recordings of various artists from the first Ozzfest concerts; Ozzy sings on one track.
Perry Mason

1997 *Private Parts*: US LP, cassette & CD; from soundtrack; Ozzy sings on one track with Type-O Negative.
Pictures Of Matchstick Men

1997 *Ozzfest Doggy Bag*: UK & US CD; Ozzy sings on one track.
Black Sabbath – Snowblind

1997 *Under Wheels Of Confusion*: UK & US 4-CD box set; Black Sabbath greatest-hits compilation; Ozzy does not sing on all tracks; 2000 digitally remastered CD reissued.
DISK 1: Black Sabbath; The Wizard; N.I.B.; Evil Woman; Wicked World; War Pigs; Paranoid; Iron Man; Planet Caravan; Hand Of Doom; Sweet Leaf; After Forever; Children Of The Grave
DISK 2: Into The Void; Lord Of This World; Orchid; Supernaut; Tomorrow's Dream; Wheels Of

Confusion; Changes; Snowblind; Laguna Sunrise; Cornucopia (Live); Sabbath Bloody Sabbath; Killing Yourself To Live; Hole In The Sky; Am I Going Insane (Radio)

DISK 3: The Writ; Symptom Of The Universe; Dirty Woman; Back Street Kids; Rock 'N' Roll Doctor; She's Gone; A Hard Road; Never Say Die; Neon Knights; Heaven And Hell; Die Young; Lonely Is The Word

DISK 4: Turn Up The Night; The Sign Of The Southern Cross; Falling Off The Edge Of The World; The Mob Rules (Live); Voodoo (Live); Digital Bitch; Trashed; Hotline; In For The Kill; Seventh Sign; Heart Like A Wheel; The Shining; Eternal Idol

1997 *The Ozzman Cometh*: UK & US cassette, CD & MiniDisc; greatest hits compilation; limited edition has second PC-enhanced CD (as listed) plus screen savers, QuickTime movies, and games.

DISK 1: Black Sabbath (Alternate Version); War Pigs (Alternate Version); Goodbye To Romance; Crazy Train; Mr. Crowley; Over The Mountain; Paranoid; Bark At The Moon; Shot In The Dark; Crazy Babies; No More Tears (Edit); Mama, I'm Coming Home; I Don't Want To Change The World (Live); I Just Want You; Back On Earth (Unreleased)

DISK 2: Fairies Wear Boots (Unreleased); Behind The Wall Of Sleep (Unreleased); Ozzy 1988 interview

1997 *The Ozzman Cometh*: US PC-enhanced double CD; as above, plus videos for Crazy Babies, Crazy Train, Mr. Crowley, I Just Want You, Paranoid (Live); also screensaver and video game in which you 'whack Ozzy's bones'

1998 *Chef Aid: The South Park Album*: CD; Ozzy sings on one track with DMX and Ol' Dirty

Bastard; three versions of CD – the others are 'Extreme' and 'Clean'. Nowhere To Run

1998 Ringo Starr: *Vertical Man*: CD; Ozzy sings on one track.
Vertical Man

1998 *The Ozzfest '98*: UK & US CD; available only at Ozzfest '98; Ozzy sings on one track.
Black Sabbath – Psycho Man

1998 *Diary Of A Madman / Bark At The Moon / The Ultimate Sin*: boxed 3-CD set; all tracks remastered

1998 Black Sabbath: *The Ozzy Osbourne Years*: UK & US CD; greatest-hits 3-CD box set.

DISK 1: Black Sabbath; The Wizard; Behind The Wall Of Sleep; N.I.B.; Evil Woman; Sleeping Village; Warning; War Pigs; Paranoid; Planet Caravan; Iron Man; Hand Of Doom; Fairies Wear Boot

DISK 2: Electric Funeral; Sweet Leaf; After Forever; Embryo; Lord Of This World; Solitude; Into The Void; Wheels Of Confusion; Tomorrow's Dream; Changes; Supernaut; Snowblind; Cornucopia; St. Vitus' Dance; Under The Sun

DISK 3: Sabbath Bloody Sabbath; A National Acrobat; Sabbra Cadabra; Killing Yourself To Live; Who Are You?; Looking For Today; Spiral Architect; Hole In The Sky; Symptom Of The Universe; Am I Going Insane (Radio); Thrill Of It All; Megalomania; The Writ

1998 Black Sabbath: *Rock Giants*: UK & US CD; greatest-hits compilation.
Sabbath Bloody Sabbath; Wizard; Sweet Leaf; Electric Funeral; Into The Void; Wheels Of Confusion; Paranoid; Iron Man; Am I Going Insane (Radio); Killing Yourself To Live; Snowblind; Hole In The Sky; Laguna Sunrise; War Pigs

1998 *Trust Me*: US interview CD

1998 Black Sabbath: *Reunion*: UK &

US double cassette & CD; Ozzy on vocals; limited-edition CD in digipak; also on MiniDisc; recorded live at the NEC, Birmingham, on 5 December 1997; Iron Man won a Grammy Award for Best Metal Performance on 23 February 2000.
DISK 1: War Pigs; Behind The Wall Of Sleep; N.I.B.; Fairies Wear Boots; Electric Funeral; Sweet Leaf; Spiral Architect; Into The Void; Snowblind
DISK 2: Sabbath Bloody Sabbath; Orchid / Lord Of This World; Dirty Women; Black Sabbath; Iron Man; Children Of The Grave; Paranoid; Psycho Man; Selling My Soul

1999 Rick Wakeman: *Return To The Center Of The Earth*: US cassette & CD; Ozzy sings on one track.
Buried Alive

1999 Coal Chamber: *Chamber Music*:
US cassette & CD; Ozzy sings on one track; this also appears on the Peter Gabriel tribute.
Shock The Monkey

1999 Busta Rhyme: *E.L.E. (The Final World Front)*: US cassette & CD; Ozzy sings on one track.
This Means War

1999 *Rock: The Train Kept A Rollin'*: US 2-CD set; heavy-metal compilation; Ozzy sings on one track.
DISK 2: No More Tears

1999 *No Boundaries: A Benefit For The Kosovar Refugees*: US cassette & CD; Ozzy sings on one track.
Black Sabbath: Psycho Man (Danny Saber Remix)

1999 *Detroit Rock City*: US cassette & CD; from soundtrack; Ozzy sings one track.
Black Sabbath – Iron Man

2000 *Loud Rocks*: LP, cassette & CD; heavy-metal compilation; two versions, one cleaned up, Ozzy sings on one track.
For Heaven's Sake (2000 Version, with Wu-Tan Clan)

2000 Black Sabbath: *Maximum Sabbath*: UK & US interview CD with color picture disk; deluxe card slipcase, 8-page illustrated booklet & fold-out poster; Ozzy only sings on some tracks.
Intro; Black Magic; Princes Of Darkness; Hard Rock Lifestyle; Sabbra Cadabra; Soul Sabotage; Death And Glory; Heaven And Hell; Dungeons And Dragons; Born Again; Headless Cross; Nativity In Black; Last Supper

2000 Black Sabbath: *Singles*: 6-CD box set; digitally remastered; in rare picture sleeves.
Wicked World; Iron Man (Vertigo Japan); Paranoid; The Wizard (Vertigo Scandinavia); Tomorrow's Dream; Laguna Sunrise (Vertigo Germany); Sabbath Bloody Sabbath; Changes (Italy 1973); Gypsy; She's Gone (Vertigo Yugoslavia); Never Say Die; She's Gone (Vertigo Spain)

2000 Black Sabbath: *Best Of (Limited Edition)*: UK & US CD; all tracks digitally remastered.
DISK 1: Black Sabbath; The Wizard; N.I.B.; Evil Women (Don't Play You); Wicked World; War Pigs; Paranoid; Planet Caravan; Iron Man; Electric Funeral; Fairies Wear Boots; Sweet Leaf; Embryo; Children Of The Grave; Lord Of This World; Into The Void
DISK 2: Supernaut; Snowblind; Sabbath Bloody Sabbath; Killing Yourself To Live; Spiral Architect; Hole In The Sky; Don't Start (Too Late); Symptom Of The Universe; Am I Going Insane (Radio); Dirty Woman; Never Say Die; Hard Road; Heaven & Hell; Turn Up The Night; Dark / Zero Hero; Tomorrow's Dream

2001 Black Sabbath: *The Collection*: UK & US CD; greatest-hits compilation.
Paranoid; Behind The Wall Of Sleep; Sleeping Village; Warning; After Forever; Supernaut; St. Vitus'

Dance; Snowblind; Killing Yourself To Live; Sabbra Cadabra; The Writ

2001 *Ozzfest – Second Stage Live*: UK & US 2-CD set; Ozzy sings one track on each disk.
DISK 1: I Don't Know
DISK 2: Perry Mason

2001 *Ozzfest 2001: The Second Millennium*: UK & US CD; Ozzy sings on one track.
Black Sabbath – The Wizard

2001 **Down To Earth**: UK & US PC-enhanced CD; video includes a 13-minute retrospective plus the 'much-sought-after footage' of Ozzy with Randy Rhoads performing Crazy Train and Mr. Crowley in 1982.
Gets Me Through; Facing Hell; Dreamer; No Easy Way Out; Something That I Never Had; You Know . . . (Part 1); Junkie; Running Out Of Time; Black Illusion; Alive; Can You Hear Them?; No Place For Angels

2001 **Black Sabbath**: *Miniatures 1970–1978: Black Sabbath, Paranoid, Masters Of Reality, Volume 4, Sabbath Bloody Sabbath, Sabotage, Technical Ecstasy, Never Say Die*:
US 8-CD deluxe box set; all packed in miniature replica LP sleeves; also includes exclusive 16-page photo booklet

2001 **Rob Zombie**: *The Sinister Urge*: UK & US digitally remastered CD reissued; Ozzy sings backup on one track; two versions of CD, one cleaned up.
Iron Man

2002 *Maximum Ozzy*: UK CD billed as an 'Audio Biography'
Intro / The Man Who Was Rock; The Young Apprentice; Storm Clouds Gather; Kings Of Oblivion; Descending; A New Beginning; Annus Horribilis; The Struggle; Goodbye And Hello Again; Back To The Beast; The Devil Rides Out; Behind The Mask

2002 *The Scorpion King*: UK & US digitally remastered CD reissued; from soundtrack; performs with Rob Zombie.
Iron Man

2002 *Blizzard Of Ozz*: UK & US digitally remastered CD reissued; bonus track *You Lookin' At Me Lookin' At You*

2002 *Diary Of A Madman*: UK & US digitally remastered CD reissued; bonus track I *Don't Know (Live)*

2002 *No More Tears*: UK & US digitally remastered CD reissued; bonus tracks *Don't Blame Me; Party With The Animals*; also PC-enhanced version and MiniDisc

2002 *The Osbourne Family Album*: UK & US CD; released on 11 June 2002; tracks selected by Ozzy and family; three sung by Ozzy (Dreamer; Mama, I'm Coming Home; Crazy Train); one sung by Kelly Osbourne and Incubus (Papa Don't Preach)

2002 *Live At Budokan*: UK & US cassette & CD; released on 25 June 2002.
I Don't Know; That I Never Had; Believer; Junkie; Mr. Crowley; Gets Me Through; Suicide Solution; No More Tears; I Don't Want To Change The World; Road To Nowhere; Crazy Train; Mama, I'm Coming Home; Bark At The Moon; Paranoid

2002 *Bark At The Moon:* UK & US digitally remastered CD reissued; bonus tracks *Spiders, One Up The 'B' Side*

2002 *Live At Budokan [Explicit Lyrics]:* UK & US PC-enhanced CD; recorded live at Budokan Hall, Tokyo, Japan on 15 February 2002

2002 *No Rest For The Wicked:* UK & US digitally remastered CD reissued; UK bonus track *Hero*; US bonus tracks *The Liar, Miracle Man*

2002 *Ozzmosis:* UK & US digitally remastered CD reissued; bonus tracks *Whole World's Fallin' Down, Aimee*

2002 *Ozzie X-Posed: The Interview:* UK & US CD

2002 *Diary of a Madman / Blizzard of Oz / No More Tears:* UK & US 3-CD box set

2003 *Essential Ozzy Osbourne:* UK & US double-CD

DISC 1: Crazy Train; Mr. Crowley; I Don't Know (Live) (with Randy Rhoads); Suicide Solution; Goodbye To Romance; Over The Mountain; Flying High Again; Diary Of A Madman; Paranoid (Live) (with Randy Rhoads); Bark At The Moon; You're No Different; Rock 'N' Roll Rebel; Crazy Babies; Miracle Man; Fire In The Sky; Breakin' All The Rules

DISC 2: Mama, I'm Coming Home; Desire; No More Tears; Time After Time; Road To Nowhere; I Don't Want To Change The World (Live); Perry Mason; I Just Want You; Thunder Underground; See You On The Other Side; Gets Me Through; Dreamer; No Easy Way Out

Films, video cassettes and DVDs chronologically

19?? *Musikladen Live (Beat Club 1969):* video cassette.
Blue Suede Shoes; Black Sabbath; Iron Man; Paranoid

1978 *Black Sabbath: Never Say Die (Live in 1978):* Video cassette; DVD issued 2003
Symptom Of The Universe; War Pigs; Snow Blind; Never Say Die; Black Sabbath; Dirty Women; Rock 'N' Roll Doctor; Electric Funeral; Children Of The Grave; Paranoid

1989 *Moscow Music Peace Festival:* video cassette & laser disk

1982 *Speak of the Devil:* Video cassette; DVD issued 2003
Over The Mountain; Mr. Crowley; Crazy Train; Revelation (Mother Earth); Steal Away; Suicide Solution; Goodbye To Romance; I

Don't Know; Believer; Flyin' High Again; Iron Man; Children Of The Grave; Paranoid

1983 *Bark At The Moon:* video cassette.
I Don't Know; Mr. Crowley; Rock 'N' Roll Rebel; Bark At The Moon; Revelation (Mother Earth); Steal Away; Suicide Solution; Center of Eternity; Flying High Again; Iron Man; Crazy Train; Paranoid

1984 *Prime Cuts: Heavy Metal:* video cassette; Ozzy sings on one track.
Bark At The Moon

1986 *The Ultimate Ozzy:* video cassette & laser disk; live and video footage of one or more shows from The Ultimate Sin tour.
Shot In The Dark; Bark At The Moon; Suicide Solution; Never Know Why (We Rock); Mr. Crowley; I Don't Know; Killer Of Giants; Thank God For The Bomb; Lightning Strikes; Flying High; Secret Loser; Iron Man; Crazy Train; Paranoid; Ultimate Sin

1986 *Trick Or Treat:* film; DVD issued 2002; Ozzy plays Reverend Aaron Gilstrom, a fanatical fundamentalist preacher!

1987 *The American Way:* film; Ozzy plays himself

1988 *The Decline of Western Civilization Part II: The Metal Years:* film & video cassette; exploration of heavy-metal music and its performers: Ozzy plays himself

1988 *Wicked Videos:* video cassette & laser disk; features 'making of' footage for first two tracks.
Miracle Man (Uncensored); Crazy Babies; Crazy Train (*Tribute* Version)

1991 *Don't Blame Me:* video cassette & laser disk; mostly interviews with Ozzy and friends talking about his career; some rare footage of Randy Rhoads; 2001 reissued on DVD.
N. I. B.; Blue Suede Shoes; Fairies Wear Boots; Iron Man; War Pigs;

Paranoid; Suicide Solution; I Don't Know; Mr. Crowley; Crazy Train; Mama, I'm Coming Home; No More Tears (Unedited Version)

1992 *The Black Sabbath Story Vol. 1*: video cassette; Ozzy on vocals. N.I.B. (Paris 1970); Paranoid (Belgium 1970); War Pigs (Paris 1970); Children Of The Grave (California 1974); Snowblind (London 1978); Sabbath Bloody Sabbath (Concept Video 1973); Symptom Of The Universe (London 1978); It's Alright (Rare Footage 1976); Rock 'N' Roll Doctor (Rare Footage 1976); Never Say Die (BBC 1978)

1993 *Live & Loud*: video cassette & laser disk; limited-edition packaging with speaker grille similar to CD; different running order; DVD issued 2002

1995 *The Jerky Boys*: film; Ozzy plays a band manager

1995–7 *Ozzy Goes To Hollywood*: video cassette; there seem to have been several versions of this comedy film, shown at the start of concerts. The limited-edition video, sold at 1997 Ozzfest concerts, 'showed visions of the Ozz Man in Hanson, Spice Girls and Fiona Apple videos as well as a clip from the movie *Titanic*, the Riverdance and many other silly situations'.

1997 *The Ozzfest*: video cassette; recorded at Phoenix, Arizona, 25 October 1996 and San Bernardino, California, 26 October 1996; Ozzy sings on one track only. Perry Mason (Live)

1997 *Private Parts*: film, video cassette and DVD; biopic of American shock-jock Howard Stern; Ozzy plays himself

1999 *We Sold Our Souls for Rock 'N' Roll*: film & video cassette; recorded on the 30-city Ozzfest '99 tour, with performances by Ozzy on vocals with Black Sabbath

1999 *The Last Supper*: video cassette & DVD; Black Sabbath: Ozzy on vocals; various running orders known.
Into The Void; Snowblind; Dirty Women; Iron Man; Electric Funeral; Sweet Leaf; Black Sabbath; Paranoid; Children Of The Grave; War Pigs; N.I.B.; Fairies Wear Boots; After Forever; Spiral Architect (Sound Check)

2000 *Little Nicky*: film, video cassette & DVD; Ozzy plays himself

2003 *Live at Budokan (2002)*: UK and US video & DVD; tracks as CD

2003 *Rockthology, Vol. 2*: US video & DVD
Episodes from 1990s US TV programme *Hard and Heavy* includes one on Ozzy

2003 *The Osbournes – The First Season (Edited)*: UK & US video & DVD
All 10 episodes of the first season with commentary; DVD bonus tracks includes un-aired footage from six episodes

2003 *The Osbournes – The First Season (Uncensored)*: UK & US video & DVD
All 10 episodes of the first season with commentary; DVD bonus tracks includes un-aired footage from six episodes, four new episodes

Ozzy Chronological

1948, December 3 John Michael Osbourne born in Aston, Birmingham, England to John (Jack) and Lillian Osbourne, the fourth of their six children

1962 Ozzy forms his first band: The Black Panthers

1965 Ozzy serves six weeks (sentenced to three months) in Winson Green Prison for burglary

1965–7 Ozzy sings briefly with Music Machine, Approach and Rare Breed

1968 Ozzy joins Tony Iommi, Terry 'Geezer' Butler, and Bill Ward to form the Polka Tulk Blues Band, soon renamed Earth. They tour in UK and Europe

1969 Band change name to Black Sabbath; they also move to a heavier sound

1970, January First demo single, 'Evil Woman', released in UK

1970, February 13 First album, *Black Sabbath*, recorded in twelve hours and released on Vertigo label in the UK

1970 *Black Sabbath* released in USA by Warner Bros. The band tours American colleges

1970, September Second album, *Paranoid*, is released in the UK

1970, September Band sack Jim Simpson as manager and hire

Patrick Meehan and Wilf Pine instead

1971, July *Master of Reality* released. Band tours again in USA

1971 Ozzy marries Thelma Mayfair; she already has a son named Elliot who is adopted by Ozzy

1972, September *Volume 4* released in UK

1972 Ozzy and Thelma have their first child, Jessica

1973, December *Sabbath, Bloody Sabbath* released in UK

1974, April 6 Black Sabbath perform at California Jam in Ontario, California

1974 Ozzy meets Sharon Arden

1975 Ozzy and Thelma's son Louis is born

1975, July *Sabotage* is released in the UK

1975, December Compilation double disk *We Sold Our Souls For Rock 'n' Roll* released

1976 Band part company with Meehan and Pine and hire Don Arden

1976, October *Technical Ecstasy* is released in UK

1977, November Ozzy leaves Black Sabbath, only to rejoin two months later

1978, January 20 Ozzy's father, Jack, dies

1978, October *Never Say Die* released.

Ozzy tours with Black Sabbath for the last time. At the end of the tour (December 1978), he is sacked

1979, March Ozzy starts his solo career, signing with Don Arden's Jet Records

1980, September Ozzy releases first solo album, *Blizzard of Ozz*

1980, September Ozzy launches UK tour with his band in Glasgow

1981, March Ozzy bites the head off a live dove at a meeting with Epic Records in Los Angeles. He and Sharon are thrown out. The publicity made the tour sell out

1981, May Ozzy launches a US tour to support *Blizzard of Ozz*

1981 Break-up of Ozzy and Thelma's marriage. They are divorced

1981, October 31 Second album, *Diary of a Madman*, released on Halloween. Black Sabbath release *Mob Rules* at same time

1982, January 20 During US tour, Ozzy bites the head off a bat on stage in Des Moines, Iowa. He is banned in Boston as a result

1982, February 19 In Texas, Ozzy arrested for urinating on the Alamo when drunk. He is banned from playing in San Antonio

1982, March 19 In Florida, a plane crash kills three including Randy Rhoads, Ozzy's guitarist and co-star

1982, July 4 Ozzy marries Sharon Arden in Maui, Hawaii

1982, Sept 26–7 *Talk of the Devil*, double album of Black Sabbath songs, recorded at the Ritz, New York to fulfill Ozzy's contract with Don Arden. Released in November

1983, May 29 Ozzy performs at the USA Festival in San Bernardino, CA for a crowd of over 350,000

1983, September 2 Aimee Osbourne is born

1983, December 2 Ozzy, now managed by Sharon, releases *Bark at the Moon*

1984, October In California, John McCollum commits suicide while listening to *Blizzard of Ozz*

1984, October 27 Kelly Osbourne is born

1984, October 28 Ozzy checks into the Betty Ford Clinic

1985, January Ozzy appears at the Rock in Rio festival in Rio de Janeiro, Brazil

1985, July 13 Ozzy reunites with original Black Sabbath members Tony Iommi, Geezer Butler, and Bill Ward to play the Live Aid benefit concert in Philadelphia, Pennsylvania

1985, November 8 Jack Osbourne is born

1986, January 13 John McCollum's parents sue Ozzy and CBS Records, claiming that listening to *Suicide Solution* drove him to kill himself

1986, March *The Ultimate Sin* is released. Ozzy starts another US tour

1986, May 2 Ozzy co-hosts NBC-TV's *Friday Night Videos* with Dr Ruth Westheimer, the sex therapist

1986, December 19 A California Superior Court judge denies a motion to reinstate the *Suicide Solution* lawsuit, citing First Amendment protection

1987, March Randy Rhoades tribute album, *Tribute*, is released

1987, early summer Ozzy stars as the Rev Aaron Gilstrom in horror movie *Trick or Treat*

1987, July Ozzy begins a six-week tour of UK prisons

1988, July 18 California Supreme Court upholds the decision to dismiss the *Suicide Solution* lawsuit

1988, October *No Rest For the Wicked* is released. Ozzy starts another US tour

1989, March Ozzy's duet with Lita

Ford, 'Close My Eyes Forever', reaches US Top Ten

1989, August 12–13 Ozzy plays the Moscow Music Peace Festival with Bon Jovi, Mötley Crüe, the Scorpions, and Skid Row

1989, September 2 Ozzy is jailed after attacking Sharon. He is released on condition that he goes into rehab for three months.

1989, December Ozzy is released and they get back together

1990, March Ozzy and Geezer Butler release live EP, *Just Say Ozzy*

1990, August Compilation album of old material, *Ten Commandments,* is released by Priority Records

1990, October In Georgia, USA, parents of two teenagers who shot themselves, blame Ozzy's music for the deaths. They start lawsuits

1990, December 16 Ozzy makes cameo appearance on US TV series *Parker Lewis Can't Lose*

1991, February 8 Ozzy plays KNAC radio station's anniversary concert in Long Beach, CA

1991, May 6 District Court judge in Atlanta dismisses the suicide lawsuits on First Amendment grounds

1991, September *No More Tears* is released

1991, September The video *Don't Blame Me: The Tales of Ozzy Osbourne* is released

1991, October 5 Ozzy headlines at the Foundations Forum convention in Los Angeles. Three weeks later, Ozzy breaks his foot on stage in Chicago. After three more shows, he postpones the rest of the tour due to an infection

1992, January 5 Ozzy resumes his Theater of Madness tour in Sunrise, Florida

1992, March 26 Randy Rhoads Memorial Concert held at Long Beach Arena, California. Ozzy says profits will build a new tomb for Randy

1992, March 28 Ozzy invites audience on stage at Irvine Meadows, Laguna Hills, California. Fans cause $100,000 worth of damages. Ozzy receives minor bruises

1992, June Ozzy starts the No More Tours tour. He claims this will be his last tour as a solo artist

1992, October 1 US Supreme Court upholds rulings that the First Amendment protects Ozzy against lawsuits alleging his music encourages suicide

1992, October 31 Ozzy takes part in ABC-TV's *Halloween Jam* at Universal Studios with the Black Crowes, Slaughter and AC/DC

1992, November 15 Concert at the Pacific Amphitheater, Costa Mesa, California ends with a Black Sabbath reunion. Tony Iommi, Geezer Butler and Bill Ward join Ozzy for a thirty-minute set

1992, November 18 Black Sabbath is honored with a star at the Rock Walk on Sunset Boulevard, Hollywood

1993, July 3 Live double album *Live and Loud* released. It was recorded at some of the No More Tours concerts

1993, October Ozzy appears on US ABC's *Halloween Jam II*

1993 Ozzy wins a Grammy Award for Best Metal Performance for *I Don't Want to Change the World*

1994, September Ozzy's *Muppet Show* duet with Miss Piggy, singing 'Born to Be Wild', is released on the children's album, *Kermit Unpigged*

1994, October Ozzy joins with Therapy? to sing 'Iron Man' on *Nativity in Black — A Tribute to Black Sabbath*

1995 Bored by retirement, Ozzy flies to Paris to record *Ozzmosis*

1995, August Ozzy launches a Latin American tour in Monterey, Mexico. This is followed by short tours in USA and Europe

1995, October *Ozzmosis* is released

1995, November–December Ozzy tours Europe

1995, December 31 Ozzy launches Retirement Sucks tour in Denver, Colorado. It ends with five concerts in Japan in March

1996, August 17 Continuing touring, Ozzy is joint lead band at the Castle Donington Festival with KISS

1996, September 14 The first Ozzfest concert held

1996, October 26–7 Two expanded Ozzfest concerts held in Phoenix, Arizona, and San Bernardino, California

1997, March Compilation album and video *Ozzfest Live!*, featuring bands from 1996 Ozzfest concerts, are released

1997, May Ozzfest '97 starts. Ozzy plays with his own band and with 'Geezer' and Tony

1997, November A greatest hits package, *The Ozzman Cometh*, is released

1997, Dec 4, 5 Black Sabbath reunited for two shows at the NEC, Birmingham

1998, May Ozzy launches a European tour with his band, plus performances with Black Sabbath

1998, June 20 Ozzfest '98 is held at the Milton Keynes Bowl in England. Then Ozzy plays four more concerts with Black Sabbath in Europe

1998, July 3 US Ozzfest '98 begins in Holmdel, New Jersey

1998, September Ozzy interviewed in *Penthouse* magazine. Book published, *Paranoid: Black Days*

with Sabbath & Other Horror Stories, by Mick Wall

1998, September 24 Black Sabbath is first nominated for Rock and Roll Hall of Fame

1998, October 18 Ozzy is featured in TV cartoon series *South Park* (Chef's Aid)

1998, October Black Sabbath release the two-CD *Reunion*, with Ozzy on vocals, recorded at a concert in Birmingham, 5 December 1997

1998, October 21 Ozzy gives a thirty-minute interview on MTV's *Revue*

1998, October 30 Black Sabbath appear on *The Late Show with David Letterman* and sing 'Paranoid' – their first live TV performance for twenty-three years

1999, February *Reunion* goes platinum: the first Black Sabbath album to do so since *Heaven and Hell*

1999, May 27 Fourth Ozzfest starts, featuring Black Sabbath. Also known as The Last Supper Tour, because it is claimed to be the last time that Black Sabbath will tour together

1999, Dec 21, 22 Black Sabbath play Birmingham, saying the two shows will be the last time they will ever play together

2000, June Ozzy plays a show in LA for KROQ radio and surprises everyone by reuniting with Black Sabbath

2000, July 31 Ozzy appears on UK TV programme *You Only Live Once* with Nick Hancock

2001, August Ozzy and Sharon buy a £4.5 million property in Beverley Hill, California. They sold their previous home for £2.5 million

2001, April 10 Lillian Osbourne dies of complications from diabetes. Ozzy is devastated

2001, May 28 Ozzfest '01 concert at Milton Keynes Bowl – Ozzy plays with Black Sabbath again

2001, October *Down To Earth*, Ozzy's first solo album for six years, is released

2001, October MTV cameras move in

2001, October *Ozzy Osbourne's Black Skies*, a PS2 3D fight combat game, is announced

2001, November Ozzy slips in the shower before a concert in Arizona on his Merry Mayhem tour and gets a stress fracture in one leg. Ten dates have to be postponed

2001, December 23 Ozzy plays an emotional World Trade Center benefit show at the Meadowlands Stadium in New Jersey

2002, March 5 First of ten episodes of a fly-on-the-wall documentary series, *The Osbournes*, appears on MTV in USA. It is a smash hit

2002, April 15 Ozzy is inducted into the Rock 'n' Roll Hall of Fame

2002, May 5 Ozzy and Sharon have dinner with President Bush in the White House, Washington DC

2002, May 10 Ozzy appears on UK TV programme *Friday Night with Jonathan Ross*

2002, May 26 First episode of *The Osbournes* appears on MTV in UK

2002, June 3 Ozzy performs at Queen Elizabeth II's Golden Jubilee Concert at Buckingham Palace, London

2002, July 4 Sharon is diagnosed with cancer of the colon after routine tests discover abnormal growths

2002, July 29 Ozzy announces he will be taking a three-week break from Ozzfest to be at Sharon's side as she begins chemotherapy treatment

2002, August 7 Ozzy returns to Ozzfest at Sharon's insistence

2002, August 13 Kelly releases her cover version of Madonna's 'Papa Don't Preach' in the US

2002, September 9 Kelly's single is released in the UK; it reaches Number 3 on September 15

2002, September 14 Accompanied by Kelly, Sharon makes her first public appearance since being diagnosed with cancer, to accept an Emmy award for best reality series for *The Osbournes*

2002, October 25 Ozzy performs live in Las Vegas, his first solo show since 1997

2002, October 27 Kelly celebrates her eighteenth birthday with a family party

2002, November 1 Channel 4 begins screening *The Osbournes* in Britain

2002, November 26 The second series of *The Osbournes* begins on MTV in America
Kelly releases her second single and debut album, both entitled *Shut Up*, in the US

2002, December 25 Sharon delivers her Alternative Queen's Speech on Channel 4 television in Britain

2002, December 31 Ozzy and Sharon renew their wedding vows live on MTV to mark their twentieth wedding anniversary

2003, January 27 Kelly's single, 'Shut Up', is released in the UK

2003, February 10 Kelly's album, *Shut Up*, is released in the UK

Ozzy Predictable

We all know of the demonic behavior of Ozzy Osbourne and much of this is reflected in his chart. He has the normally harmonious planet Venus in Scorpio, the sign of death and transformation. This placing of the planet means he pursues the black side of human nature and is fascinated with the macabre. But is he the devil incarnate or simply an impish prankster?

PERSONALITY

Ozzy's sun sign is Sagittarius, the fun-loving sign of the zodiac. Never taking life too seriously, Sagittarians crave freedom, enjoy life to the full and have a great sense of humor. However, ruled by Jupiter, the planet of excess, they believe in doing everything on a grand scale. Consequently, they can be irresponsible, over-indulgent, and often like to make practical jokes at others' expense.

Versatility is another quality of the Sagittarian, but this can cause them to be disorganized and lacking in perseverance. Tending to over-estimate their abilities, they are tempted to promise more than they can deliver. They enjoy being involved with many different things at the same time, but are often unable to complete any of them. Fortunately, Jupiter is also the planet of luck, and they frequently seem to have plenty of it on their side, helping them to achieve where others might fail.

Sagittarians' optimistic outlook and enthusiasm for life means they rarely allow disappointments to get them down. Any failures they may experience are quickly put behind them and they move on to the next great adventure. However, optimism leads them to take risks, and elsewhere in Ozzy's chart there are strong indications that he is accident-prone. A less boisterous approach to life would be advisable, and he should be more cautious. Fortunately, Sagittarians often acquire wisdom late in life, choosing to adapt to challenges rather than fighting them.

The Sagittarian risk-taking characteristics in Ozzy's chart are offset with influences from his Moon in the sign of dependable Capricorn. This particular Moon placing often indicates a child from a poor family, who would have had to take the mother's place because she was working, or emotionally absent. Certainly she would have been a strict disciplinarian and the controlling influence in the family, but also dependable and hard-working. However, this Sagittarian/Capricorn blend also means Ozzy possesses many underlying contradictory characteristics. He is unorthodox but also a traditionalist. Although he is a maverick, there is a hidden desire for self-control and respect, and his impulsive actions are often curbed by desires for material security. He is like an uncontrollable child trying to escape from a wise old soul.

Ozzy's child-like boundless energy is emphasized through the Sun's link with the planet of communication, Mercury. He makes decisions hastily, often ignoring other people's advice. In his desire to make a dramatic impression he always has to have the last word, and finds it difficult to say sorry. The problem with someone born under this Sun/Mercury combination is that they fail to recognize that their opinions are not necessarily the only answer, and that others may have more valid ideas. If he could be more objective and less forceful in his approach it is likely that he would meet less resistance. However, having a fertile imagination, he is brimming with ideas and stimulates those around him with enthusiasm.

Ozzy's Mercury makes a particularly stressful connection with Saturn, the planet representing limitations and restrictions. Traditionally this would indicate somebody who has come from a large family where so much is going on that they find it difficult to be heard. Perhaps one parent didn't notice him at home, and subsequently he now needs to be noticed, and when he isn't, he feels insecure. This would account for his reliance on alcohol and drugs. It could also be that he was ignored at school because teachers wrongly assumed he was stupid, and he consequently became lazy. Undoubtedly he was accused of talking too much in class, and maybe he was even criticized for the way in which he talked. This has led him to believe that other people are more articulate or intelligent than him. He therefore constantly tests himself by pushing the boundaries, as well as using his outrageous behavior to test his audience. This planetary combination is typical of somebody who totally rejects the voice of authority, and is perceived by society to be an oddball.

Ozzy is an individual living on the edge. The close link with warring Mars and excessive Jupiter in his chart means that he has no understanding of fear, even in the face of danger. Constantly taking chances and tempting fate, he enjoys rising to a challenge and revels in the subsequent publicity. He has total conviction in the things he fights for, and his belief that he can get away with anything means that he frequently does. However, carelessness does, at times, get him into hot water. Fortunately, Mars makes a particularly beneficial, if rather weak, link with restricting Saturn, thus moderating his actions. It is, however, something he has to work at. Hopefully, the restraining effects of Saturn should also warn him of situations that could be harmful to both him and to those around him.

Saturn is the educator of the zodiac, and there is much Ozzy should have learnt from his foolish actions in the past. Foolhardy behavior is indicated in Ozzy's natal chart where Mars and Jupiter rebelliously join up to confront Uranus, the planet of the unexpected. The extremely stressful opposition of these planets makes him hyperactive and wilful, and he allows nothing to stand in his way. Stubbornly objecting to any form of restriction, tradition or authority, he will fight for freedom, often with dramatic consequences. However, this planetary alliance brings originality and resourcefulness, allowing him to wriggle out of tight corners. Also, Jupiter's beneficial qualities with this opposition to Uranus in a chart can bring about sudden strokes of luck, which have proved fortunate in the past.

HEALTH

Many of the influences from Ozzy's Sun sign and from Mars and Jupiter account for an excessive lifestyle. Love of food and drink means that regular exercise is essential, and a healthy diet should be followed.

Undoubtedly, with Ozzy's strong Mars/Jupiter/Uranus mix he is very accident-prone. Traditionally, Mars/Jupiter is associated with getting injured in fights and also scalding. A Mars/Uranus connection is far more dangerous, as it encourages acts of impetuous exhibitionism. Desperate to receive the approval of others, and often in too much of a hurry to pay due attention to his safety, accidents inevitably happen. Ozzy should definitely avoid taking risks, or acting hastily. However, such advice probably would be met with as much ingenuous disregard as a child being told a fire is hot.

RELATIONSHIPS

As a Sagittarian, and having strong independent feelings, Ozzy needs space in a personal relationship. If not exactly a philanderer, he would rebel against any restrictions inhibiting his freedom-loving spirit. Between the sheets, inhibitions are abandoned with exuberance, and with his strong Mars/Uranus influence, he probably likes to get there quickly.

A Sun/Saturn conflict in his chart indicates that people shouldn't take him too seriously, particularly when he is joking. He wears the face of the clown, and uses that mask as a defense mechanism. It might be that he is frightened of exposing the real Ozzy Osbourne.

He may often be seen by others as cold and detached. With his Moon in Capricorn he has difficulty expressing his emotions and finds it impossible to relax. Although he is generous with his affection and recognizes responsibilities, it is important that his partner allows him time to concentrate on his own needs.

With Venus, the planet of romance, in the intensely jealous

sign of Scorpio, relationships will never be easy, with frequent emotional upheavals. He would enjoy a love fight and is certainly attracted to the strong, independent type. Regardless of how unobtainable or unsuitable the object of his desires may be, he would pursue them with passion. Should anyone cross him in love, revenge would be sought with equal intensity. However, despite the fact that one minute he may be sizzling and the next icy, he will always live up to his moral obligations and remain loyal.

WORK AND CAREER

The Sun's awkward position with Saturn, the planet of work, in Ozzy's chart indicates someone who has to experience several failures before they achieve success. Surprisingly, he seems to have had a low opinion of himself in his youth and underestimated his potential. Fortunately, as he has got older these feelings should have faded. However, the stressful link between Mercury and Saturn still occasionally produces strong negative emotions and a fear of challenges, and he will be tempted to go away and hide.

The normally aggressive Mars makes a sympathetic link with his Saturn, helping Ozzy to organize his time when pursuing creative endeavors. With Jupiter also in perfect alliance with Saturn he doesn't expend his energy on unimportant matters. Others may think that he has been lucky in his achievements, but he knows that he has had to work hard for them. Past feelings that he wasn't good enough have spurred him on to achieve and make his mark.

Ozzy could have a tendency to become apathetic to success, but this would be a mistake. There are indications in his chart that he has the ability to pursue a totally different career later in his life. His greatest strengths lie in encouraging other people to achieve, and he would be highly effective in some kind of public post promoting education.

INFLUENCES FROM HIS PAST

1977 through to 1978 was undoubtedly a bad time for Ozzy Osbourne. At the age of twenty-nine he was experiencing for the first time in his life the effects of transiting Saturn connecting with his natal Saturn. He would have experienced changes that he found disturbing, but, allowing for other influences in his chart, he probably ignored them. With Saturn also making stressful challenges to his natal Sun and Venus, both material things and people would have disappeared from his life, and relationships would have come under stress. From August to October 1978, with Jupiter challenging his natal Jupiter and then Mars, there were considerable disagreements involving work. Towards the end of 1979 through to the beginning of 1980, as transiting Jupiter connected with his Saturn, he broke completely free of all responsibilities and finally ended a relationship.

Ozzy has experienced a number of other challenging periods in his life. When Randy Rhoads died on 19 March 1982, transiting Uranus was squaring up to Saturn in Ozzy's chart. Uranus brings about sudden changes and Saturn represents the foundations of our lives, and his certainly would have been severely shaken. In Randy Rhoads' chart, transiting Jupiter was squaring up to Uranus, creating a need to be free from restrictions – or a desire to fly off into the sunset. Also, transiting Uranus was clashing with his natal Saturn, leading to uncharacteristic, sudden actions. This may account for why Rhoads decided to take the fateful plane trip, despite his fear of flying. It is no coincidence that, at the time of Rhoads' death, Ozzy was experiencing a major planetary influence which can only happen approximately once every forty-two years.

In 1984, Ozzy went into the Betty Ford Clinic, when Saturn, planet of reality, was making contact with elusive Neptune. Under this planetary combination he would have experienced negative moods, and the temptation to resort to drugs or alcohol to boost his confidence would have been very strong. Also, with transiting Neptune opposing his natal Uranus, causing doubt and confusion, it would have been a period of tremendous instability. Fortunately, Uranus was taking up a particularly advantageous position to Ozzy's Sun, enabling him to break free from his emotional difficulties.

Ozzy is entering a deeply significant and exciting period of his life. The planet of revolution and change, Uranus, which is so important in his chart, is taking up a crucial position to his natal Uranus, which will bring about further changes in the direction in his work. Providing that he can resist the temptation to fight against the restrictions confronting him when Saturn curbs his energy in the autumn of 2002, and again in the early summer of 2003, this will be a successful period. However he is in danger of upsetting people around him during those periods, and consequently could end a relationship or an important contract. Ozzy should take particular care of his health during these times, and not take any risks while his energies are low.

Ozzy will be presented with even more unusual opportunities in 2003, and it is quite possible that his life will take off in a totally different direction, bringing greater personal satisfaction. As bizarre as it may seem, there are indications elsewhere in his chart that he eventually will work closely with children, and 2003 could be the year when he makes the move. The most likely period would be from September to October. Again, it is important he nurtures relationships at this time and also takes care, as he could be accident-prone.

His biggest change will come when he reaches his mid fifties in 2004. Before then, he will have opportunities to restructure his life and prepare himself for the future. It is vital that he uses this time to lay down solid foundations, because in 2005 he will face restrictions, and may experience financial setbacks. By 2007 and 2008 he will certainly have left the life of rock and rollercoaster rides far behind.

ADRIAN MORRIS, 2002

Ozzy's Tattoos

'I've got so many tattoos that I look like a road map.'

Ozzy's interest in tattoos began in childhood. He was fascinated by his grandfather's tattoo of a snake that went from his head all the way down to his toes. He acquired his first tattoo as a teenager in jail and others were added over the years, many when Ozzy was on the road on tour. Bored with sitting in his hotel room, he would pick up the local *Yellow Pages*, find his nearest tattoo parlour and book an appointment. Yet Ozzy was horrified recently, when his seventeen-year-old daughter Kelly came home with a tiny heart tattoo on her left hip. 'Kelly, you've got that there for the rest of your fucking life!' he exclaimed.

Ozzy now has more than fifteen tattoos, including:

His first tattoo, the world-famous OZZY on the knuckles of his left hand, which was done with the aid of a needle and the lead from a pencil

Two smiling faces – one on each knee – designed to cheer him up when he woke every morning, applied by the same method in jail

The number 3 on his right arm, acquired during his time in jail, using a tin of grey polish, which was melted and stuck into the skin with a needle

A knife and a heart on his left arm applied in jail using grey polish

A stick man figure on his left wrist

A skull with a knife through it on his left arm

A long pointed dagger with an Ozzy banner on his left arm

A woman's face on his upper left arm

A bat on his left shoulder

A red-hooded ghoul on his left chest

A blue dragon with red flames on his right chest

A rose on his right upper arm with the word Sharon tattooed underneath it

A leaf design underneath his right arm

A Mom and Pop tattoo on his right arm, now obscured by a red and blue swirling pattern, which covers most of his right arm

A dagger on his left thigh

Index

236